THE PREVENTION AND TREATMENT OF ABORTION

THE PREVENTION AND TREATMENT OF ABORTION

Frederick Joseph Taussig

General Books

www.General-Books.net

Publication Data:

Title: The Prevention and Treatment of Abortion
Author: Taussig, Frederick Joseph, 1872-1943
Reprinted: 2010, General Books, Memphis, Tennessee, USA
Publisher: St. Louis : C.V. Mosby compny
Publication date: 1910
Subjects: Abortion
Bisac subject codes: FAM014000, LAW043000, MED033000, REF004000, SOC046000,

How We Made This Book for You
We made this book exclusively for you using patented Print on Demand technology.
First we scanned the original rare book using a robot which automatically flipped and photographed each page.
We automated the typing, proof reading and design of this book using Optical Character Recognition (OCR) software on the scanned copy. That let us keep your cost as low as possible.
If a book is very old, worn and the type is faded, this can result in numerous typos or missing text. This is also why our books don't have illustrations; the OCR software can't distinguish between an illustration and a smudge.
We understand how annoying typos, missing text or illustrations, foot notes in the text or an index that doesn't work, can be. That's why we provide a free digital copy of most books exactly as they were originally published. You can also use this PDF edition to read the book on the go. Simply go to our website (www.general-books.net) to check availability. And we provide a free trial membership in our book club so you can get free copies of other editions or related books.
OCR is not a perfect solution but we feel it's more important to make books available for a low price than not at all. So we warn readers on our website and in the descriptions we provide to book sellers that our books don't have illustrations and may have numerous typos or missing text. We also provide excerpts from each book to book sellers and on our website so you can preview the quality of the book before buying it.
If you would prefer that we manually type, proof read and design your book so that it's perfect, simply contact us for the cost. We would be happy to do as much work as you would be like to pay for.

Limit of Liability/Disclaimer of Warranty:
The publisher and author make no representations or warranties with respect to the accuracy or completeness of the book. The advice and strategies in the book may not be suitable for your situation. You should consult with a professional where appropriate. The publisher is not liable for any damages resulting from the book.
Please keep in mind that the book was written long ago; the information is not current. Furthermore, there may be typos, missing text or illustration and explained above.

1

THE PREVENTION AND TREATMENT OF ABORTION

MY FATHER
   THIS BOOK IS AFFECTIONATELY
   DEDICATED.
   PREFACE
This book is addressed primarily to the general practitioner, to "whose lot it falls to treat the vast majority of abortions. I have tried to be clear and exi licit in my instructions as to methods of preventing abortions, and as to operative indications and operative technique, and trust the reader will not hesitate to let me know in what respect I have failed to answer the questions that come up for consideration in his practice.

I wish to express my thanks to Dr. Philip Skrainka and Dr. A. E. Taussig for assistance with the text, Dr. R. E. "Wobus for his kind help with the illustrations, and Dr. G. Gellhom and Dr. H. Ehrenfest for helpful suggestions. My thanks are also extended to Dr. H. S. Crossen for permission to use a number of cuts from his Text-book on Diseases of Women, and to Messrs. Wni. Wood Co. for a similar obligation.

I am likewise indebted to Prof. R. J. Terry for permission to use some of the specimens of the Anatomical Museum, Washington University, for i)urposes of illustration.

The Prevention and Treatment of Abortion. Frederick Joseph Taussig

Many of the original drawings were made by Mr. Ivau Summers, to whom I wish here to acknowledge my appreciation of his interest. A tinal word of gratitude to the publishers for their friendly cooperation.

Metropolitan Bldg. November, 1909.

VIU COXTKNTS.

Page

Diagnosis of Stago of Almilion 41
Diagnosis of Incomplete Abortion 43
Diagnosis of Duration of Pregnancy 47
Diagnosis of Cause of Abortion 48
Diagnosis of Criminal Abortion 48

CHAltl R VII.

nifferpntial Diagnosis 50 Irregular Menstruation 50
Hemorrbagii- Endometritis 50
Submucous Fibroid 51
Carcinoma of the Uterus 52
Tubal Abortion 53

CHAPTER VIII. Prognosis 58

PART II.

PrfAENTION of AlloRTION.

CHAPTER IX.

Prophylaxis Before Conception 61
Retroverted Uterus 62
Wassermann Reaction 65

CHAPTER X.

Prophylaxis During Pregnancy 67
General Measures 67
Syphilis 68
Other Causes 69
Habitual Abortion 73

CHAPTER XI. Prevention of Threatened Abortion 75

CHAPTER XII.

Prevention of Criminal Abortion 78
Education 79

COXTEXTS.

PART in.

Tbeatment.

CHAPTER XIII.

Page

Treatment of Uncomplicated Abortion-

CHAPTER XIV.

85 After-treatment

CHAPTER XV.

Operative Indications

CHAPTER XVI.

Instrumentanum 91 Special Instrument Case
Self-retaining Speculum
CHAPTER XVII.
97 Operative Technique 97 General Preparations 99 Expression of the Ovum
Vaginal Tamponade 101 Uterine Tamponade
Cervical Dilatation 107 Dilatation with the Bag 109 Digital Removal
Removal bv Placental Forceps 1
Curettage
Ecouvillonnage"
Intrauterine Douche ""
CHAPTER XVIII. Complicalioub and Their Treatment Hemorrhage 123
CHAPTER XIX.
127 Retained Placenta
Outline of Treatment
CHAPTER XX. 133
Sapreniia
Mild Sepsis . 130)
Severe Sepsis 137 Local Measures Injections Into the Blood
Operative Treatment
CHAPTKR XIX.
Page
Perforation 144
Syniptoins 146
Diakiiosis 14G
Cause and Prevention 148
Treatment 150
APPENDIX.
Missed Abortion 152
Treatment 154
Mole Pregnancy 156
Fleshy Moles 156
Hematoma Moles 157
Hydatid Moles 159
Therapeutic Abortion 168 Incarcerated Pregnant Uterus 162
Hyperemesis 163
Maternal Diseases 163
Narrow Birth Canal 165
Technique 165
Prevention of Conception 166
Ergot and Its Preparations 167 INTRODUCTION

Since T. Gaillard Thomas published his series of six lectures on "Abortions" in book form, in 1895, tliere has not appeared in the English language any monograph dealing in a comprehensive way with this important subject. During the fifteen years that have elapsed since that time many changes have occurred in our knowledge of this branch of obstetrics, and it has seemed to me a favorable moment to attempt a resume of the present ideas regarding the cause, irevention and treatment of the premature expulsion of the human ovum. The text-books on obstetrics have, to be sure, taken up this question as one chapter in their general field; but only too frequently. I might even say universally, the consideration given it is not at all proportionate to the importance of the subject. Abortions and miscarriages compose a very considerable percentage of all pregnancies (one in five according to most authors); yet only a few books devote more than 30 pages out of 1,000 to their consideration. The mortality after abortions is higher than that aftei-confinements. Complications involving operative measures occur with far greater frequency, and every gynecologist knows what a large proportion of his patients date the onset of their trouble to a mismanaged abortion. It is a far more serious condition than we formerly considered it, and demands our most careful consideration and analysis.

The writing of this monograph, therefore, has been undertaken in the ho ie that the general practitioner might gain the essential facts as we know them at present, and might be guided to a selection of the form of treatment suitable for the case in hand. In thus outlining a plan of treatment I have tried to avoid, as much as possible, injecting my own personal views to an undue degree. Conclusions are based upon a critical consideration of the experiences of all European and American obstetricians. Merely to state the opinions of these obstetricians, without trying in a way to pick the

J ixTKOnrctTOX.

grain rniin the cliiilt, would rt'sult in iiroducinn- a confused impression ujion the readci-. On tlie contrary, 1 luive felt it my duty to 1)0 ratlur delinite in my instiuctions, since the book is intended jirimarily for the jiractitioner. Wliile it is, therefore, more of a critifal review of the subject than a collci-l ion of personal experiences, J iia c ti-icd to iclicvc the severity of the text by citing an occasional conci-ete cxainiile in illustration of the jioint T wish to make. Some fifteen or more selected histories have thus been quoted from among my personal observations.

Although the title of tlic monograph throws the emphasis on "Prevention and Treatment," these could not be thoroughly understood without at least a l)rief review of the anatomy, pathology, etiology and diagnosis of this condition. Hence tlie lirst portion of the book is devoted to these matters. In the concluding chapters I have considered cot a in correlated topics, such as mole pregnancy, missed abortion, tli(ra)ientic aboi'tion, etc.

Definition. Aiiortion is the pre vialtle expulsion of the liuman ovum. Ahortion occu))ies the same relationship to the first six months of itreguaucy that labor does to the last three months. It will be noted that the tei-nis al)ortion and miscarriage are used synonymously. Some have tried to differentiate between them in accordance with the stage at wliicli pregnancy is interrupted abortions in tlie first three months and miscarriages from the fourth to the sixth month but this seems an unnecessary complication. In general the tei-m I have preferred is abortion, since, despite the odium attaching to the name, it more ii-op(rly defines the condition.

Frequency of Abortion

The rapidh growing uiunber of ubortious, both mstrumental and spontaneous, has of late been the occasion of much discussion among sociologists, particularly iu its application to the Malthusian theoiy of over-population and the relative decrease of population in France as compared with Germany. Just what influence such a diminution iu the number of inhabitants will have on the prosperity of the nation is a moot question, but statesmen in many countries see in it a national danger.

A few years ago Doleris published statistics regarding the increase of abortions in France, which caused the state authorities gieat anxiety and induced vigorous measures to be taken to limit criminal abortions. Doleris found in certain of the poorer districts of Paris that the number of abortions had doubled and even trebled from the years 1897 to 1905. That a similar increase of abortions has occurred in other countries there seem little reason to doubt.

The statistics on abortions are very difficult to gather, since many cases are neither treated in institutions nor even receive medical attention.

The figures of the Paris Maternite from 1897-1905, as collected by G. Rimette, show 9,875 pregnancies, 1,437 abortions, 627 spontaneous abortions, 414 complicated abortions, 367 infected abortions, 27 deaths from abortion.

licli; iil(rr, wild l); is('s his liii-iircs nil Iaz. USS birtlis in one of the liussinii niatcniitics. Juiiiid Ihnt tlic jnninniion of abortions to full-ternl deliveries was aliiiit 1 to lu. Keyssuer, in his polyclinic 7natoriai, found 46!) nborlions to li,()23 eonlinenionts, or 1 to 5.6. The figures of iio. spitals are bound to be too low, since they omit the numerous cases that are taken care of at home. Even the records of polyclinics, whore tlic ihysi(ian attends tlie patients in their homes, do not give a complete estimate as to freciuency, for many mothers have an abortion with hardly an untoward sym)tom and absolutely without medical attention.

As Chazan points out, the only accurate statistics are those obtained by (nestioning the mothers directly on this matter. The evidence thus far at hand from such sources is very insufficient. For this reason I undertook the labor of looking over the clinical records of the last 600 patients treated in the gynecological clinic of the Washington University ITos iital. 1 found that out of these 600 women 348 had been pregnant. Of this number tiiere were 87t) full-term pregnancies in 293 patients, 371 abortions in 201 patients, 36 confessedly instrumental abortions, 50 women who developed some gynecologic disease after abortion.

This would make the ratio of abortions to confinements 1 to 2.3.

The relative frequency with which abortion occurs in accordance with the stage of i regnancy has also been the occasion of statistics. Kueise found that out of 500 cases abortion developed

During the first month in 6 cases, During the second month in 157 cases, During the third month in 222 cases. During the fourth month in 73 cases, During the fifth month in 37 cases, During the sixth month in 5 cases.

statistics obtained from general medical clinics where the anamnesis is carefully recorded ought to be even nearer the truth than those I have obtained from gynecological sources. At any rate the comparison would be interesting.

This corresponds apjiroximatel. y to the figures giveu by other writers. It seems certain that a very large percentage of the abortions occurs during the latter half of the second and the whole of the third month. The decidedly greater frequency at this period, according to Thomas, is due to the following reasons: (1) The nutrition of the fetus is undergoing a radical change at this time.

(2) The placenta is now rapidly develoiing- and thereby caus- ing marked circulatory changes in the uterus.

(3) Syphilis is at this time most apt to affect the fetus.

(4) Retroversion is most apt at this period of uterine develop- ment to cause pressure symptoms.

I should be inclined to take exceptions to Thomas's statement relative to syphilis, since this disease causes fetal death, and hence abortion, iisually at a. somewhat later period than the third month. Furthermore, I should be inclined to add as a reason for tlie frequency of abortions at this time the fact, that usually it is not until the second period has been passed, that women feel so siire of being n-eguant as to be willing to submit to instrumental interference. This reason seems esidecially weighty when we consider the fact that such criminal instrumental interference is probably the direct cause of almost 50 per cent of all abortions. It is always difficult to obtain a confession of such a criminal act from a patient. My own figures, 36 out of 371 abortions (10 per cent), are about what Treub found in his first series of statistics (202 criminal out of 1,924). In 1907 he paid especial attention to this point in getting histories from his patients and found as a result 52 instrumental out of 218, or 25 per cent. No doubt the actual number is even considerably higher than this. Of the criminal abortions 105 were in unmarried and 97 in married women.

Abortions of all sorts occur more frequently among women who have had children than among those who have not. Franz found in 844 cases, only 41 primiparae. Furthermore, most women who have had one abortion are liable to have several more. In my own list I find record of many women who had from 8 to 10 abortions. In such cases the rule was that they were brought on instrumentally. In the case of women who wear an infra-uterine pessary the number of abortions that are thereby produced artificially is difficult to esti- iiijili", siiuo (lioy (KTur at such an early stage as liaidly to bo dil'ter-entiatod tvoiu delayed inenstiiiatidii. In one of the cases of mole ir(i; iiancy rc i(iite(l l)y me in lhOi. the i)aticnt j ave a history of hav-iiii; liad lour abortions in one ycai-. These figures would doubtless be even larger were it not for the great deterrent factor of)elvic inflammation which in time almost invariably attacks tliese women. Either by sealing the tubes or by producing an atrophic or hypertrophic endometritis it eventually prevents further conception.

Anatomy of Early Pregnancy It is only by a true appreciation of anatomical con- ditions in the first half of pregnancy that we can arrive at an understanding of the pathology and correct management of abortions, i s the ovum develops, its circula- tory conditions change radically. These changes are of course gradual ones, but are sufficiently marked at certain periods to permit of a division into three stages:

Stage 1. The first six weeks of pregnancy. Stage 2. From the sixth week to the end of the twelfth week. Stage 3. From the twelfth to the twenty-fourth week (fourth to sixth montli).

In accordance with the special anatomical conditions in each of these three stages, interruption of gestation will result in a pax-ticular manner of expulsion. The treatment will also be different for each stage, since the mechanical factors to be considered vary greatly.

Stage 1. Period of Implant a t ion i n V t e r us a n d Formation of Intervillous Spaces. Chorion a n d I) e c i (1 n a over entire Circumference of 0 V u m. A m n i 0 t i c C a i t y Small. 0 v u m a bout 1 cm. long, sharply bent, so that Head and Breech almost touch. No rmhilical Cord.

The spermatozoon, after an interval ui hours, days or weeks, subsequent to its ejaculation into the vagina, having come into direct contact with a mature ovum, impregnation occurs, usually near or in the fimbriated portion of the tube. Several days, however, elapse until this impregnated ovum reaches the uterine cavity. In the second half of the first week of pregnancy this ovum, about 1 mm. in diameter, bores its way into the uterine nuicosa which is already in a state of active hyperemia, and becomes imbedded there. Dining

Ajstatomy of early tregnancy. y these first two weeks the greatest activity is manifest in the outermost layer of embryonal cells the trophoblast. These trophoblastic cells multiply and eat their way into the distended maternal capillaries surrounding the ovum. Thereby blood spaces arise, growing more and more considerable in extent, until at the end of the second week the ovum is no longer intimately connected with the maternal tissues, but is separated from them by a layer of blood spaces. The trophoblast has by this time changed from a mass of proliferating cells into that tree-like branching structure known as the chorion, the center of its stem being connective tissue, the outer surface a double layer of cells. Of these cells the inner layer is called the Langhans layer, and the outer one, syncytium. The term "syncytium"

Figure 3 Sagittal section of two halves of uterus in early pregnancy (5-6 weeks), showing especially changes of consistency in the uterine wall. (Edgar, after Pinard.) is used because the cells are not separated from each other, but are fused into one web-like band with many separate nuclei of various sizes and shapes. At the same time the maternal tissues have also become altered. Together with the dilatation of the blood vessels there has come about a peculiar swelling or growth of the connective tissue cells of the mucosa, termed decidiia formation. These decidua cells are usually very large, about 20 to 50 microns in diameter, varj greatly in shape, and have a delicate protoplasm that usually takes a slightly blrush stain with haematoxylin. Their nuclei are also large, usually round in shape and do not stain deeply.

Accoidiiii; ti its positinii. ifi.-it i c to the (i uni, llic dccidiia formed in the utci-iiic inufosa l)cais a dinvrciit iiainc. I'lie decidual lajer situated at the base ol the site ol iiui)laiitatiou is called decidua basilaris, or scrotiiia. The decidua covering the ovum at this point is called decidua capsularis, or rdcxa. The decidua fornuml in the mucosa outside the site of iniiilanlation is termed decidua Iera. There is also a marked proliferation of the uterine glands in the lower layers of the mucosa, so that the latter may be divided into an upper compact layer consisting almost wholly of decidua cells decid. ua compacta) and a more deeply situated layer of a spongy character (decidua spongiosa), in which there are but few decidua cells and a great many proliferating hypertrophic glands.

Decidua-iici-i

Figure A Ovum in situ of about four weels' development, showing tile formation of the decidua vera, with the reflexa covering the ovum. (Bumm.)

As seen in Figure 4 the cavity of the uterus during the first six weeks is only partially filled by the growing ovum. Decidua reflexa and vera do not touch each other. The uterus itself is enlarged from the size of a pear to that of an orange. The depth of the uterine cavity increases from 2 12 inches to 3 12 inches or more. The embryo by the end of the first month has already developed the beginning of its most important organs. Head, trunk and extremities are differentiated. The amniotic cavity during these weeks begins to fill with fluid and to enlarge at the expense of the exo-coelom cavity. This causes the amnion to be pressed more closely about the blood-vessels leading from the chorion to the fetus, wherebj there is formed at this point a cylindrical band called the umbilical cord.

Stage 2. From the 6th to the 12th week. Period of Placental Formation. Fixation of Ovum by Villous Stems to Uterus. Ovum 3 to 8 cms. long. Cord Present. Amniotic Cavity Comparatively La r g e.

After a period during which the ovum is but loosely attached to the uterus, there ensues at the end of the sixth week a rapid

Placenta Orif. inf. uteri furies recti
Vesica iiriii
V. (lorsalis cl riirnis: ragin. post.
I, spiiitcter a I) I ext.
funua miiscid, recti
Clitoris I M. sphincter aiii ext.
I Urethra
Tunica muscul. urcthr. Vagina

Figure 5 Frozen section of female pelvis in a case of three months' gestation, showing marked anteflexion of pregnancy. (Waldeyer.) rulvKNTIoN AND TKEATMENT OP ABOHTION.

extension ol e-lioiioiiic villi iuto the surroundiug maternal veins. The openings of these veins into the primary intervillous spaces are dilated by this growth, so that new venous spaces are thus produced. This dilatation takes place at the expense of the surrounding tissue. Figures tj-7 give a diagrammatic sketch of these changes. Laterally the branches of the villous stems become imbedded in the tissues about the maternal blood vessels so that the ovum is again tirmly attached to the uterus. Between these points of firm attachment lie the so-called secondary intervillous spaces just described, in which the maternal blood now circulates in larger amount, to supply the growing fetus with sufficient nutrition. The decidua reflexa grows in extent by the splitting off of the upper part of the compact layer of the decidua vera surrounding the ovum. By this lateral de-

Figrure 6.
Figure 7.
Figures 6-7 Diagrammatic sketch of tlie formation of the primary and secondary Intervillous spaces. In Figure 6 we see the chorionic viilous stems iying in the primary Intervillous spaces with their tips just entering the maternal veins. In Figure 7. tile villous stems liave already dilated the veins, thus forming the secondary intervillous spaces. C. V. = Chorionic Villous Stems; I. S. = Intervillous Spaces; V. = Maternal Veins; A. = Maternal Arteries.

velopment of the ovum a portion of the vera is converted into reflexa, a portion into basilar decidua. The growth of the chorionic villi at the point of implantation results in a partial absorption of decidua. At the conclusion of the twelfth week the placenta has been completely formed. On the other hand, over the reflexa portion of the ovum there is during this period an obliteration of the primary intervillous spaces, so that the chorion lies in direct apposition to the decidua reflexa. Ordinarily we speak of this portion of the chorion as chorion laeve, or smooth chorion, whereas the portion at the base or insertion of the ovum, owing to its branching, is termed the chorion frondosiim. The amniotic cavity develops considerably in size during these six weeks. The amnion is pressed closely against the chorion as the cavity becomes dilated with fluid, and the umbilical cord begins to lengthen as the fetus is given greater room for movement. The embryo during these second six weeks be- comes mucli less bent. The head develops so as to be larger than the body. The extremities become articulated. The abdomen protrudes, owing to the growth of the liver. The external ear becomes noticeable. External genitals gradually develop and differentiate by the

Abganpstcllc dcr Occ. rellexa

Membrana Chorij

Oric. Cit,

Figure 8 Pregnant uterus of three months' gestation, showing the development of the membranes and decidua and their relationship to the uterine cavity. Eihohle = Amniotic Cavity; Uterushohle Uterine Cavity. (Bumm.) twelfth week into male and female. The umbilical ring is closed. Beginning ossification takes jilace. The uterus, which was as large as an orange at the end of the sixth week, becomes as large as a pineapple by the twelfth and is increasingly softer and more globular. The lower uterine segment is distinctly formed.

Stage 3. Fri. iii I lie IJtli to I lie I-Mli Week. P(M-io(l of 1 fa f 0 I11 a I (I III w til. () li I i 1 c r a j i n ii (i I l)e c i d ii a Reflex a.

After tlio twelftli week the placenta, which providiisly had its edges turned in, assumes a Hatter aiipeaiance and grows in extent as tlie uterus itself grows larger. Its thickness increases at the expense of the spongy layer of the deeidua basilaris. At the sixteenth week the diameter of the jilacenta is 10 to 11 cms. and its thickness 12 to 1 cm. At the twentieth week the diameter is 12 to 1o cms. and the thickness about 2 cms. At the end of the twelfth

Figure 9 Cro-ss-section of female pelvis with five months' gestation. (Crossen, after Eflgar.) week the placenta occupies only about one third the surface of the uterine cavity, whereas its extent at the twentieth week is over one-half of this surface.

Histologically, we note the disappearance of the inner layer of chorionic epithelium known as Langhans cells. There remains only the syncytium separating the chorionic connective tissue from the maternal blood spaces. In the maternal placenta we have during this time the beginning of fibrinous areas due in all irobability to de, a: ederation of decidua. Bom the sixteeuth-n-eek ouward the decidua refiexa is in direct contact with the decidua vera. In other words, the original uterine cavity is completely obliterated and the uterus entirely tilled by the ovum. The two layers of decidua lying tlius in apiktsition become agglutinated and degenerative changes take place in the reflexa until by the twenty-fourth week the latter has completely disappeared, and the ehorio-amnion lies directly upon the decidua vera.

The fetus develops rapidly in size duriug these months. Its skin begins to be covered with lanugo. The external genitals assume their characteristic form. The eyelids, nostrils, mouth and anus become open. The urinary tract develops and the intestines contain a greenish meconium. Centers of ossification progress rapidly. Tlie uterus enlarges during this period of twelve weeks, growing from an organ barely j erceptible above the sym ihysis into one tilling the entire lower half of the abdomen and extending to the umbilicus. Its softness is mucli luore marked, including both the. cervix and the vaginal wall.

Pathology of Abortion

Depending upon the state of its anatomical development as just described in Ciiaplor Tl, tlie iiianner of expulsion of the ovum varies greatly.

(1) During Sta e I (the first six weeks), the usual course is for the entire ovum with its decidua, to be expelled intact (Fig. 10). It

Figure 10 Six weeks' ovum expelled with its membranes and decidua intacti The ovisac has been cut open. (Enlarged 2X.) (Specimen In Anatomical Museum, Washington University.) is also rather common at this period to have the ovum extruded from its decidual sack, with which it is but loosely connected (Fig. 20). The ovum in this event appears as a globular body with shagg exterior. The decidua is expelled later en masse or piecemeal. As a rule, in these earlj" cases, the decidua comes away as one piece and not rarely it is a cast of the uterine cavity: a triangular body with the internal os and the tubal comers indicated by open-

PATHOrx)GY OF ABORTIOX.

Lags. It will be recalled that from the second to the sixth week of gestation the ovum is surrounded by blood-spaces and has no deep, firm connection with the maternal tissues. Hence its complete expulsion is the rule. The decidua, which just about equals the ovum in bulk, likewise comes away as a whole, ordinarily. "When this does not happen it may have to be removed with the finger. A form of exijulsion that occasionally takes place during this period is for tlie chorion and decidua reflexa to break open and thus permit the fetus, covered by its amnion, to escape. The chorion and decidua are then usually expelled together. It happens every now and then that a idortion of the chorion adheres like a cap to the glistening amniotic sack.

Figure 11 Embryo and ovisac of two months' development, showing the moss-like character of the chorionic villi. The amnion has been peeled from the chorion and is wound around the insertion of the umbilical cord (Case No. 7). B = Embryo; U. C. = Umbilical Cord; A = Amnion; C. V. = Chorionic Villi; C. L. = Chorion Laeve.

During Stage II, of ovular development, the process of expulsion is usually somewhat different. Owing to the inward growth of the villous stems, the chorion is firmly attached to the uterine mucosa. Hence, even if the ovum is expelled without rupturing the membranes, there is, as a rule, some chorion and decidua left in the uterus. It is during this period that we are most likely to meet with retained portions of placenta. The fetus may be hanging out of the rrEVEXIKin AM) IKIvaIM KXI OK AHOKTION.

iitonis with llie cntiic iil; ic(iit; i still; i(lhcr(nt. This is j; n liciiiarly iipt to be the case where iiistniiiieiits have hecii employed to induce aliortioii. and llie nicinliraiics llicicli luptarcd. Where tlio membranes ai-c intact the cximilsivc iiaiiis ahuic will ordiiiarilv not suffice

Figure 12 Decidual cast from same case as Figure 11. D. B. = Docicuia Basilaris; D. C. = Decidua Capsularis.

to break them. Tlie decidua may be adiierent to tlie chorion or it may come away as a shreddy discharge in tlie week following niis-

During Stage III, from the twelfth to the twenty-fourth week, tlie manner of expulsion of the ovum resembles more and more that of full-term labor. There is a period of cervical dilatation, often extending over weeks, followed by the rupture of the membranes and the expulsion of the fetus. The latter will usually be found hanging by a slender umbilical cord to the still adherent jdlacenta. The placenta, which, as its development progresses, is more readily separable from the uterus, usually is expelled entirely, shortly after the fetus has come away. The placenta is expelled more slowly during this period than after labor at term: (1) because the uterine contractions of the earlier months are less powerful; (2) because the cervix is less fully dilated, the placenta being as a whole larger than the fetus, and hence requiring a greater degree of dilatation; (3) because there is at this time a closer connection l)etween ovum and

Figure 13 Fetus of (our months' gestation lying intact in its amniotic sac. Chorion and Jecidua retained. U. I. = Umbilical Insertion. (Specimen in Anatomical Museum, Washington University.) uterine mucosa, especially when, as is frequently the case, the two have become more closely adherent as a result of inflammatory processes.

Occasionally, as in one of my recent cases (Fig. 14), the entire ovum is expelled with the amniotic cavity still intact, but this is the excei:)tion. The Iule is to have three stages of expulsion similar to the three stages of labor at term.

Figure 14 Intact ovum of five months' development expelled unruptured (Case 8). Owing to the method of preservation and to light reflection, the photograph does not show the 25 cm. long fetus lying within the amniotic cavity. The placenta lies to the left and above, covering about one-half of the ovisac.

So much for the pathology of abortion as a whole. Let us now consider the special pathology of the products of abortion. These maj be treated under three heads: (A) Fetus.

(B) Membranes.

(C) Decidua.

A. Fetus. Many are the changes undergone by the fetus in cases of abortion. In the early weeks, when it is still to be termed embryo, it is rare that it is perfectly fresh at the time of expulsion. The usual course is for the embryo to be necrotic and greatly softened, so that it is a shapeless jelly-like mass. Not rarely the entire embryo is absorbed while the ovum is still intact. Such an event is particularly likely to happen in cases of delayed abortion and mole pregnancy. In the latter class of abortion ova, we frequently find the embryo (1 to 2 cms. long) deformed into a hardly recognizable cylindrical body.

In abortions from the third to the sixth month the fetus undergoes somewhat different changes. The fetus is too large and too bony to undergo complete liquefaction.

After death has occurred necrotic changes usually take place rapidly. Particularly is this the case if the amniotic cavity is no longer intact so that bacteria of one sort or another can gain entrance. If these are saprophytes there may be rapid decomposition, with a foul, odorous discharge. Gas-producing bacilli at times cause such bloating of the fetus as to interfere with its expulsion from the uterus.

Maceration was at one time thought to be pathognomonic of syphilis, but now we have ample proof that this is not true. Although macerated fetuses of this period are usually syphilitic, there are many exceptions to the rule. Maceration varies in degree according to the duration of the process. The first stage is marked by the formation of large blebs under the skin. Next there is a desquamation of the epithelium in large masses, starting at the point wliere the blebs formed. Finally, we have a general softening of all the joints and tissues so that the fetus loses its shape, and becomes transformed into a reddish brown raw-looking mass. In this stage it is called fetus sanguinolentus.

IlikVK. NJlo. N AM) IlikAI. MKAl' OL AliuHTloN.

r. Membranes, ratliogenic cliangos in the iiicmbraiios may bo tl io to: (1) C i r e u 1; i t o v y disturbances.

(2) Degenerations.

(3) Infectious.

(4) Tumors.

(1) ( )t tlu circiilaldr disturliaiiccs the most inijioi-tant is the so-calledacri(at of lcvy. in wliirli there is a large extravasation of blood at some jjoint in tiie memhranes, usually in tlie intervillous spaces. Such extravasations of blood, wlieu they become organized, cause pressure-necrosis of the surrounding ihi and, in this way, together witl: a blocking of the placental l)loo(l stream, interfere with the nutrition of the ovum and uuiy eventual cause an abortion. Thromlutsis of the maternal or fetal vessels sometimes occurs.

.2; ::–.:–?

Figure 15 Placi-ntal iiifaict. in which the chorionic epithelium (a) lia. s undergone hyaline degeneration except at the point marked b, where the epithelium is still intact. The chorionic connective tissue has also undergone degenerative changes. (. Winchel.)

(2) The anemic or zchitc infarct was described as early as 1648 by Guillemeau. It was formerly supposed always to be associated with pathologic conditions in the pregnancy, but later it was found to be, as Eden saj's, "a part of the normal life-history of the placenta;"

and the etiology was to be sought "in the operation of the natural lorces of evolution and decay." Where, however, the infarctions are numerous and extensive, they are often attended by maternal albuminuria. Williams says that marked infarction of the placenta in tlie earlier months is usually associated with syphilis, tuberculosis, iieiiliritis or other maternal cachexias. Abortion usually results. Calcareous degeneration is very commonly found, especially in cases of retained placenta, missed abortion or mole pregnancy.

(3) Iiihaiiniation of the chorion or placenta takes place rather frequently. A true purulent infection is not so rare as might be supposed and is usually the direct result of instrumental abortion. The septic process spreads into the decidual septa and

occasionally affects the chorion. The latter is more apt to be infected in the early months when the chorion is not so well protected by fibrinous deposits. The villus in these cases resembles a small abscess cavity and its epithelium is merely a degenerated band.

Of the non-suppurative infections of the placenta syphilitic changes occur with greatest fre(uenev. Now that it seems certain

"V-:-C: y mm:- -".-. v,, "-,— v-:: L-

Figure 16 Syphilitic placenta showing marl ed proliferation of chorionic connective tissue and reduction in size of intervillous spaces. Compare with normal placenta, Figure 19. (von Winckel.) tliat we have found the specific micro-organ ism of this disease the si irochaeta pallida it is possible to distinguish with greater certainty between those changes that are due to syphilis and those that are merely accidental. Thus infarcts were at one time thought always to be specific in origin, but are now known to occur in normal j)lacciit! U. flu sy))liiliti(i)ln(onta is iisdally Inrgcr iuid licavior and contains loss blood tliau the iioniial one. Microscopically, too, tiie villi ai pear swollen and show few branches. We see the connective tissne rci)laccd liy hirnc, round cells, whose irolitcrai ion has partially blocked tiie linnen of the blood vessels. The latter also show a marked thickeniny- iiarticulaily of the intinia. This fibroblastic proliferation of the chorion stroma is analogous to the interstitial inflammation of other organs. In conse(inence of this thickening of the illi. the inltmxillous sj aces arc much smallci, so that, as shown in Fig. 10, the picture is very different from the iioiiiial one. Tuberculosis may likewise directly alfecl the i)lacenta and produce there typical tubercles. In a certain number of cases it causes fetal death and abortion.

(4) We sliall have occasion, under the liead of Mole Pregnancy, to take uj) that peculiar proliferation of chorionic epithelium resulting in hydrops of the connective tissue, and hence known as hydatid mole. There occurs also the malignant chorio-epithelioma, or chorioma, developing from the fetal epithelium, left in the uterus after an abortion or mole pregnancy. Of other tumors we need only mention cysts of the amnion or chorion, and angiomata. These are but rarely found.

C. Decidua. Pathologic changes in the decidua occupy a comparatively important place, since during the first few months the decidua is of considerable extent. As a rule, it undergoes necrosis after the expulsion of the ovum and is absorbed or liciuefied. At other times the piocess is not so sinijile. Large portions of it may be retained, and become infected. Such a suppurative dccid. u. itis may extend to the deeper tissues of the uterus and finally cause a general sepsis. At other times the jwocess of li(uefaction necrosis of the decidua does not take i)lace and the decidual cells remain a long time in the mucosa, giving rise to a chronic hyperplastic deciduitis. In general, this is characterized by an overgrowth of either the interstitial or the glandular portion of the decidua. AVarthin believes that the cause is usually a pre-existing endometritis. We may also have a jiolypoid form of decidual hyperplasia, so-called dcciiluilis polyposa. Where a small bit of placenta is still adherent, there may be at this point, beside the decidual proliferation, a collection of blood, parth organized, partly fresh, giving rise to what is termed a placental polyp. In cases where the decidual hyperphisia is primary, it may so interfere with fetal nutrition as to cause fetal death, and thereupon an abortion. Subinvolution or cndouictritis post-abortuin is the name given to the retention of the decidual tissue without proliferation. Such a persistence of the decidua, according to some writers, takes place only when portions of the membranes have been retained. Decidual cells may be found, either as islands in the upper layers, or surrounding the blood vessels in the deeper layers of the mucosa. Glandular hyperplasia is almost always present, so marked at times as to resemble an adenoma. There has been considerable discussion between Opitz and Hitschman, the former claiming that this marked glandular proliferation was found only where pregnancy had recently occurred, the latter denying this and citing-instances of simple endometritis in which he found such a condition. In Warthin's oi)iniou abortion in the early weeks of pregnancy without thorough curetting, is almost always followed by subinvolution of the decidua, and this in turn by chronic hyperplastic glandular endometritis.

CHAitEK i-

Etiology III most text-books the causes of abortion are considered in a ery luisysteinatic and illogical way. Some consider them in the order (if their frequency (syphilis, endometritis, trauma). Others divide them into maternal, paternal and ovular causes. In fact, there is usually a loudeucy to group the causes as if al)ortion were an abnormality in the development of the ovum, whereas it is really an abnormality of the pregnant uterus.

Abortion is but a slight variation of a physiological action of the uterus. The only difference between it and normal labor is the fact that it occurs during the first half of pregnancy, whereas labor sets in at the termination of pregnancy. We should not confuse the various conditions that cause the death of the fetus with those that cause abortion. They are separate entities, each with a special etiology.

While in general the causes of abortion are those stimuli or irritants that stir up premature uterine contractions in the gravid uterus, we must differentiate between conditions of the uterus which predispose to such an expulsion of the ovum (predisposing causes) and conditions which directly excite the uterus to get rid of its contents exciting causes).

Of tlie predisposing causes of abortion we may have; 1. Increased sensitiveness to nerve stimulation a. Temperament.

b. Frequent abortions at rapid intervals.

c. Menstrual period.

2. Greater tendency to placental thrombosis, due a. To endometritis.

b. To congestion of the uterus, under which head may be mentioned constipation and coitus.

3. Lessened resistance to expulsion a. Cervical tears.

b. Amputation of cervix.

It is necessary to consider separately the predisposing causes of abortion, since the slightest mechanical or other irritation may in susceptible individuals cause a miscarriage, whereas in persons not so predisposed they would have absolutely no effect. The predisposing causes mentioned in this classification are undoubtedly a factor in many instances, but they are of secondary importance compared with the primary exciting causes.

These are: 1. Mechanical Irritation.

2. Thermic Irritation.
3. Toxic Irritation.
4. Nerve 11-1 i t a t i o n.
5. Death of the Fetus.

Of these five stimuli to uterine contractions, that of fetal death demands a word of explanation. It is grouped separately, partly because of its great importance, partly because the manner in which fetal death sets up uterine contractions is not thoroughly understood. It seems likely, however, that by partial separation of the placenta in these cases the ovum becomes, so to speak, a foreign body in the uterus and the uterine muscle is, therefore, stimulated to expel it. In this sense we might include death of the fetus under the head of mechanical irritation applied to the inside of the uterus.

It will, doubtless, strike the reader that the classification suggested in this chapter requires the consideration of certain diseases and conditions under several of the five heads already mentioned. Thus, for instance, cholera of the mother might act either as a toxic irritant, as a mechanical irritation to the mucosa of the uterus by the foimation of hemorrhagic exudates, or by causing the death of the fetus. A further objection to any classification would also be the fact that in many instances we know that certain conditions are frequently associated with abortions, but do not know the manner in which they produce them. While I willingly grant that what we do not know concerning the causes of abortion is far greater than what we do know, I believe that a logical, and hence, in this case, a physiological, i-lassilication is tlie only one lliat will Ivor create order out of tiie)reseiit cliaos, and nit us in the vay ol fiuding out the causes oi almntion in i cncial. and its cause in any partii-idar case uuder consideration. Corollary llicrt'to is. of coiii'se. the fact tlmt the jirevention of al)ortion depends luiniarily on a coriect understanding and appreciation of its causes.

Let us now try to systematize the exciting causes under their live main sub heads:

Mechanical Irritation

This may fake the form of

B. Direct Ir r i t a t i i)u.

A. Transmitted mechanical irritation is tlial in which th(uterus is not directly touched in any way. Thus we may have 1. A blow.
2. A fall.
3. A prolonged jarring, as in horseback riding, dancing or a railroad journey.
4. Straining, as in lifting lieavj objects or when the bowels are constipated.
B. Direct irritation may be applied to 1. The outside of the uterus.
2. The inside of the utei-us.

That a plied to the outside may result from traction or pressure, as when there are adhesions to the uterus, where there is a malposition crowding it into a corner of the pelvis, or where tumors of one sort or another impinge upon its growth upward into the abdominal cavity. Furthermore, outside irritation may be due to direct manipulation, as in case of a laparotomy for appendicitis, ovarian tumor, etc., or to the almost direct manipulation employed in a bimanual examination.

Direct irritation to the inside of the uterus may be due to stretching (as in acute hydramnios); to direct instrumentation, as when a sound, bougie, gauze or other foreign object is ajiplied to its interior; to the irritatiou of an exudate or liemorrhage into the endometrium, not uncommon in certain infectious fevers; and to intra-uterine tumors as in libroid polyp.

Thermic Irritation.

This may be in the form of extreme heat or extreme cold, either of which, as is well known, will stimulate the uterine muscle to contraction. This form of uterine irritation is, however, not often a cause of abortion. It may be apjjlied to the entii-e body or to the uterus alone. As an example of the former, we might mention the taking of cold sea baths. An illustration of the latter is the hot vaginal douche or the hot-water bag. AVe also hear of patients who, after an absence of menstruation for six weeks, take a hot sitz bath and thereby bring on a bleeding which they think is the normal menstruation, but which may be really an early abortion.

Toxic Irritation. This may be of three kinds: a. Chemical toxins. 1). Bacterial toxiiis. c. Placental toxins.

The chemical toxins may be certain drugs called emmenagogues, which seem to have a direct infiueuce upon the uterine muscle. They are jnimarily ergot and its associated compounds, hydrastis. styp-ticin, etc. The by-products of diabetic metabolism, the chemical substances circulating in the blood in chronic lead poisoning, and the various conditions productive of a greatly increased amount of carbonic acid gas or an insufficient oxygenization of the blood, all may be classed uudei this head of chemical toxic irritation. An illustration of the way in which an excess of carbonic acid gas in the blood is productive of abortion is given by Thomas. He relates the story of an Arab tribe who, being pursued by their enemies, were compelled to take shelter with their wives and children in a subterranean cave. Here they remained for several weeks nearly suffocating for lack of fresh air. A very large percentage of the women who were)regnant at the lime aboited during this trying-period.

, V very Jii li lovi-r is inodikiinc ol utcriiit contractions, owing to the accumulation ol carlion dioxide gas in the blood. Heart disease in the stage ol incoinpeteucy and certain diseases of the lungs have a sinular eifeel.

Bacterial loxiitx. There can be no (uestion but that many infectious diseases of tlie motlier, such as smallpox, measles, etc., stimit-late tlie uterus to contraction, owing to the toxins circulating in the blood.

Placental toxins. AVc linve now learned to consider chorea gravidarum, hyper-emesis, echunijsin, ind acute yellow atrophy as essentially similar conditions, all due to i)lacental toxemia. Any one of the four, lint Jiyperemesis in i. irticnlar. may give rise to an abortion.

Nerve Irritation.

Nerve irritation oi the uterus)roducing abortion may be classed under two heads, psychic and reflex.

Psychic nerve irritation is not an iidrequent source of abortion, but does not occur as often as many women believe. Just as, in the case of maternal impressions, the explanation follows the occurrence of the deformity, so in the case of abortion mothers are apt to ascribe it to some external mental excitement when in i-eality the premature expulsion was due to the death of the fetus. As instances of psychic nerve irritation can be mentioned fright, mental shock of any kind, severe pain as in the extraction of a tooth.

Reflex nerve irritation is in all likelihood transmitted along the sympathetic system. Vltluiugh we really know very little about such reflexes, it would ajjpear from clinical observation that they do occur. The nursing mother who, despite the fact that she is nursing her child, has become pregnant is often first led to think of such a possibility by the fact that whenever she nurses her child it starts up uterine contractions and occasionally a slight bloody discharge. Applications made to the nose have also been known to cause abortion.

Finally, every gynecologist has learned from experience tluit operative measures or, even to a certain extent, local treatment applied to the external genitals, is attended with such great risk of causing an abortion that whenever the measures necessary are rather severe, it is deemed advisable to wait with treatment until after pregnancy has been concluded.

Death of the Fetus.

Death of the fetus would seem to be the most frequent cause of aboi'tiou, just as it is the most difficult to avoid. I have subdivided this occurrence into five heads:

A. Congenital Inanition.
B. Congenital Deformities.
C. Interference zi. ith Nutrition. I). Infections.
E. Hypcrpyre. ria.

A. Congenital Inanition. Death of the fetus may be due to conditions preceding or shortly subsequent to the impregnation of the ovum. The general physical condition of the father, together with the effect of wasting diseases, alcoholism or of too frequent coitus, may result in a lowered vitality of the spermatozoon so that while impregnation may take place and the ovimi even become unbedded in the uterine mucosa, its life is soon cut short and an abortion results in the course of time. In a similar way the ova of the mother, owing to her physical condition, may be congenitally so weak as to interfere with development.

B. Congenital Deformities. The percentage of monstrosities in the ova of abortion is very considerable. Of course, the monstrosities must be of such a character that they directly interfere with the life of the fetus, otherwise development would continue. The cause of the monstrosity may be either primarily in the ovum or secondarily due to amniotic adhesions. It seems not unlikely that these adhesions form during the first months of pregnancy, before the amniotic cavity has become distended with fluid.

C. Interference ztith Nutrition. The nutrition of the embryo may be interfered with by 1. Maternal, 2. Placental or 3. Umbilical causes.

On the part of the mother, anemia, tuberculosis or similar conditions, may so interfere with her own nutrition that that of the fetus is necessarily likewise affected and its death occasionally results.

Tlio phui'iita. the most iiiii)i)rtiinl oriaaii in ivtal iiietabolisiu, is not infrequently llic site of iiiiiectious and degenerative processes. These may form necrotic areas of oriiani. cii licuiatoniata or that pecnliar n"oliferation of the fetal ei)itlieliuin known as hydatid mole formation, and so, of necessity, limit the surface area of l)lood aeration and the al)sor ition of nutritive nuiterial fi-oin the iiiotlier. Whenever such placental throniliosis or dej eneration in ol es tlie greater part of tlie phicenta, death of the fetus is almost sure to i-esnlt.

Finally. vc have interference with fetal nutrition due to an obstruction in umhilical circuhntion. Such obstruction nniy be in the Ioiin either of a tiue knot, or, in younger embiyos, of a twist through several circles of the umbilical cord. Anmiotic adhesions may also cause a constriction of the cord, with death of the fetus.

D. Infectious Diseases of the Fetus. Infectious diseases of the fetus are probably the most frotjuent cause of abortions, since we include under that head fetal syi)liilis. The great prevalence of this disease, together with the frequency with which it is ti-ansmitted to the fetus, thereby producing fetal death and abortion, has led not infrequently to tlie diagnosis of syphilis merely from the fact that a woman has frequently aborted. Even where there are no past or present manifestations of the disease, many believe that anti-syphilitic treatment should be tried in cases of repeated abortion. The results of such treatment would seem to support the view that syphilis may thus covertly attack the fetus without visibly affecting the mother.

Other infectious diseases of the fetus are directly transmitted through the i)lacenta from the mother to the fetus. They are smallpox, cholera, anthrax, plague, typhoid, erysipelas, scarlet fever, pneumonia and tuberculosis.

E. Hyperpyrexia. It has l)een mentioned that a high fever may cause toxic irritation of the uterus by the accumulation of carbon dioxide gas in the blood. When we realize the fact that the temperature of the fetus within the uterine cavity has been proved to be approximately one degree higher than that of the mother, and when we likewise take into consideration its lesser vitality, it is not surprising that a high fever, even when due to such a comparatively con-tiollable disease as malaria, may result in the death of the fetus.

Siiiiiiiiiary of Classification. Predisposing Causes: 1. Increased sensitiveness to neive irritation (temperament, fre- quent abortions, menstrual period).

2. Greater toudency to i)lacental thrombosis (inflammation of endometrium, congestion).

3. Lessened resistance to expulsion (cervical tears, or amputa- tion). F xciting Causes: 1. Mechanical Irritation

A. Transmitted (blow, fall, dancing, railroad journey, lift- ing heavy objects, constipation).

B. Direct (1) To outside of uterus (adhesions, malposition.

tumors, examination, laparotomy).

(2) To inside of uterus (instruments, hemorrhagic exu- dates, hydramnios, tumors).

2. Thermic Irritatioji

A. General (sea batli).

B. Local (hot douche, sitz bath).

3. Toxic Irritation

A. Chemical toxins (ergot, carbon dioxide, lead poisoning).

B. Bacterial toxins (maternal smallpox, measles, etc.).

C. Placental toxins (hyperemesis, chorea, eclampsia).

4. Nerve Irritation

A. Psychic (fright, pain, shock).

B. Reflex (external genitals, breast, nose).

5. Death of tlie Fetus

A. Congenital Inanition (illness of parents, alcoholism, too frequent coitus).
B. Congenital Deformities (primary iii ovum, amniotic ad- hesions).
C. Interference with Nutrition.
(1) Maternal (anemia, tuberculosis).
(2) Placental (mole degeneration, thrombosis).
(3) Umbilical (twisted cord, true knot, constrictions).
D. Infectious Diseases (syphilis, smallpox, typhoid, pneu- monia, etc.).
E. Hyperpyrexia.

Symptoms and Clinical Course

Bleeding and f ain are the caidiiial syiuiitoins oi aboi'tion, but they vaiy greatly iu character and severity, either depending upon whether the abortion is tlireatened or inevitable; or upon tlie duration of piegnancy, in other words, upon the stage of development of the fetus.

Threatened Abortion. At the onset of an abortion, certain symptoms appear so as to warn us of the impending danger, and many times are we thus enabled to save the fetus by checking the expulsive contractions. These symptoms are dragging pains in the back, a few colicky pains in the lower abdomen, a feeling of uneasiness, increased frequency of micturition, and the passage of bloody mucus or watery discharge. At this time the bleeding is not marked, there being usually only a red or brown tinge to the discharge. To some extent, however, this varies with the cause of the abortion. If an instrument has been used or a blow received, there is usually quite an active hemorrhage at the very onset.

Inevitable Abortion. When the measures to cheek contractions prove ineffectual, al)ortion becomes inevitable. The clinical api ear-ance of this condition is marked primarily by bleeding and pain. I'lie uterine bleeding which is ordinarily the earliest symptom of abortion may be continuous or intermittent. The rule is that the bloody mucus noticed in threatened abortion becomes more and more profuse until finally a few small clots of blood appear at intervals. This tendency of the blood to clot is of diagnostic value. In younger ova the bleeding is more profuse than in older ones. It is also more severe when the abortion follows quickly upon the death of the fetus than where some time has elapsed. In multiparae we have more bleeding than in primiparae. The blood is lost for the most part during the expulsion of the ovum. The hemorrhage is, however, Iarely so profuse as directly to cause the death of the mother, though she may indeed be pale and faint from loss of blood.

The pains in inevitable abortion are quite seveie, almost con- tinuous in the earlj mouths, iutermitteut iu the hiter mouths. They may compel the patieut to lie dowu, but rarely are so bad as to necessitate morphine or an anesthetic. When they are intermittent they often have the character of true labor pains, with intervals almost free from discomfort, a premonitory feeling of bearing down and then a marked cramp-like contraction pain in the lower abdomen. The pains usually persist until the uterus has entirely emptied its contents, so that the cessation of pain in a woman who is abortiug is an indication that the ovum has in all likelihood been expelled from the uterus into the vagina.

In the normal clinical course of an abortion, fcicr is not present. Nevertheless, it is found far more frequently than during the normal puerjderium. Infection is less frequently the occasion of this rise of temperature than decomposition. Such decomposition-fever results from the absorption of chemical substances into the blood from the retained decidual tissues or placenta. It varies greatly in severity, starting at 99 to 100, going up to 10.3, or in the true infections to 105 or more. AVhen the fever is high it is almost always preceded by chills or chilly sensations. The pulse is usually less varialile than the temperature. After operative measures have been employed in these cases, such as curettage, digital removal of placenta, etc., there is often a decided rise in the temperature, followed by a fall even more sudden, with free perspiration. Naturally, the frequency of unclean instrumentation and of retained placenta increases the number of infected cases.

Since there is usually considerable general disturbance of a toxic or nervous origin resulting from abortion, we have at times such symptoms as headache, thirst, weakness and vomiting. Thomas lays considerable stress on vomiting as a symptom, but others do not seem to have observed it very often. Should there be an associated septic infection we have more severe symptoms; abdominal pains, tympanites, torpor, jaundice, etc.

Physical Examination. In threatened abortion we find, besides the signs of pregnancy, a brownish vaginal discharge; occasionally a few small clots; a cervix that shows some slight dilatation, and a uterus that is firmer than the pregnant uterus of the same size.

In inevitable abortion the vagina is often filled with clots or there may be a foul, bloody discharge. The finger can be introduced into the cervical canal, since the latter has been dilated; and at the in- iiii; i; ri(i axu thkai. m kxi' oi Aiidiriio. v.

teriinl os or i)i-o, j(. ctin, n into the ciuial; i iorti()ii of the oviun can be Ielt. Whether it he niciuhiaiics, fetus or phieenta, will dei)eii(l n ion the stiif e of abortion fiinini; wliidi the examination is nia(h. The uterine liody Ieels rat her iiiiii, ami hecoines e en liriiier (hiinit; a contraction pain. Its sha))e is spherical and the lowei- uterine segment is still markedly boggy.

Iaridtioii acconhiig to the tlurtilitni of prcginiiicy. n abortit)n dur ing the first month of gestation can l)e attended by such a slight

Figure 17 Cervical abortion (Case 1). In the diagrammatic figure to the left the ovum (O) is seen still partially attached to the cervix, the internal os (I. O.) dilated and the external os (E. O.) still closed. To the right is drawn the ovum enlarged IVi times. E. = Embryo; O. = Ovum.

discomfort at times as to be overlooked, or rather interpreted as an irregular menstruation. In doubtful cases all clots must be examined. During the second month expulsion of the ovum en bloc, as a whole, is the rule. The bleeding is more pronounced. During the third and fourth months, if the membranes are intact, expulsive jiains are more violent and the ovum may be expelled in toto. The rule, however, is that the membranes are not intact, and the ovum is expelled piecemeal During the liftli and sixth mouths it has the oliuical features of a coufiuemeut. The placenta is expelled after the fetus and usually without any excessive bleeding.

Cervical Abortion. It ooeasionally hajipens, iiartirulnrly in l riniiparac, that the external os otfers such resistance to the premature exijulsion of the ovum as to lead to its retention in the dilated cervical canal for days or even weeks. This has been termed cervical abortion. The characteristic findings on examining such a patient are a small cervical opening, a globular and i-ather large cervix, above which lies the contracted uterine body. The bleeding is usually very moderate in amount, but persistent. The ovum is usually found lying free in the cervical canal, but occasionally a secondar-implantation occurs.

Subjectively the patients usually feel perfectly well. They have only bloody discharge and occasional annoying pains in the lower abdomen. There is nofoul-smelling discharge, nor any syniiitoms of decomposition except where internal examinations have been made.

Case No. 1. Mrs. B., aged 34, gave a history of having given birth to four children, unattended with difficulty. She had had two miscarriages. Menstruation had usually been regular and painless. In February it was normal. In March it was much scantier in amount, so that she suspected a pregnancy. On April lotli, one week after the expected time, she had a slight bloody discharge associated with occasional crami)iug pains in the lower abdomen. There seemed to be a slight thickening on the right side when she first consulted me on April 16th. I enjoined absolute rest in bed. not feeling-certain as to the diagnosis between extra-uterine pregnancy and threatened abortion. A few days' observation could exclude the former as a possibility. In s iite of rest and sedatives, the bleeding continued, so that on April 2'2i. there being dilatation enough to admit one finger and a mass to be felt within the cervical canal, digital extraction was determined on. This was accomplished with surprising ease. The ovum was found to consist of a in; iss the size of a walnut, loosely attached to the wall of the cervical canal, wliih above it the uterine cavity felt perfectly smooth and cni)ty. There was practically no bleeding when this ovum was removed. Figure 17 gives a direct copy of the ovum in this case, and also indicates its location in the uterus. A gentle curettement was done after-M aids. The recovery was uninteri-ui)ted.

Diagnosis

The diagnosis of abortion, in the majority of instances, is so easy that it is made by the patient lierself. At otlier times it becomes one of the most puzzling problems in gynecological diagnosis. When we recall the frequency of abortions, it will be readily appreciated tliat the total inimber of these puzzling cases is very considerable. The general practitioner will tind that a mistake in the diagnosis of al)ortion is rarely pardoned, because the laity do not appreciate this difliculty, and because the evidence of the doctor's mistake is before them with a certainty not obtainable in other conditions. Hence, he must be doubly careful in his examination and doubly guarded in his statements. Again and again, the most experienced obstetricians have been mistaken in thoir diagnosis of abortion.

Diagnosis of Pregnancy. Hand in hand with the difficulties of diagnosing an abortion is the difficulty of diagnosing pregnancy. In the early months this is often an extremely difficult task, sometimes even impossible. Without going at length iuto the description of the early signs of pregnancy, mention must be made of the amenorrhoea, morning sickness, increased sensitiveness and enlargement of the breasts, formation of cholostrum in the breasts, together with the enlargement aud softening of the uterus. The last-named sign is practically certain in nulliparae. The characteristic balloon shape of the uterus, together with the change in consistency, the softening to obliteration of the lower uterine segment, and the succulence of the cervix, leave but little room to doubt the existence of a pregnancy, especially where the patient has been examined some months previously when conditions were normal. Nariation in consistency during examination is also one of the most positive of the early signs. Bluish discoloration of the anterior wall of the vagina and of the cervix has also diagnostic value. The absence of menstruation, where there are no complicating factors such as lactation, anemia, obesity, etc., is a fairly positive sign. It is usually the first symptom that makes the patient think herself preg- naut. And yet it is a sign that must always be discounted when not suppoi-ted by the findings on physical examination. Especially would 1 warn against the positive diagnosis of pregnancy in fat women, for in them the ameuorrhoea and gastric symptoms may be due to the obesity, and moreover, the physical signs about the uterus are practically ini ossible of palpation.

Diagnosis of Abortion, (hanted that the fact of pregnancy has been established with reasonable certainty, upon what do we base the diagnosis of an abortion? First of all, u)ou the bleeding, irregular as to onset and amount, lasting far beyond the usual menstrual

Figure 18 Hegar's sign, the softening of tile lower uterine segment of the uterus during pregnancy, (Bumnt) period, and attended with clots. In the next place upon the pains, characterized by their rhythmic progression, radiating from the lower abdomen to the extremities. Pains alone, however, are frequently found in pregnant women who have previously had pelvic inflammation or endometritis, so that it is of diagnostic importance only when associated with bleeding. Digital examination will reveal the presence of clots, in greater or less amount, filling the vagina. The cervix will, as a rule, show some degree of dilatation, depending upon the stage of abortion during which the examination is made. It may hajipen that a portion of the ovum may be palpated at the external os in process of being expelled. Bimanually, the uterus lias no luniicr the suit consistency oi tlie piegnuut organ, but is quite firm owing to the continued contractions. Owing to this hardness the outlines ol the oigan become more distinct. At times, in abortions of the fourth or lillh mouth, the course of a uterine contraction can 1m" (iliscrved by tlie examining hand.

Should the (luestioii of pregnancy bo in tloubl, the diagnosis of abortion becomes miu li moi-e difficult. We must of course try to disconci the vaiious factors Iha might throw light upon the existence of a gestation. However, this is a matter of considerable diagnostic difficulty, since during al)ortion the physiological succulence and softness of the)regnant uteius has to some extent disajipeared. There is some diminution in the size of the ntei-ns. In the second montli of gestation the aborting uterus may feel almost as firm as a normal one.

Where the previous history and the physical examination leave us without a clew, we can often draw positive conclusions by investigating the charactei- of the material expelled from the uterus. Unfortunatel, women do not realize the importance of saving such l)ieces for the inspection of the doctor. Too often we are met with the reply that they were thrown away as of no consequence, or we must be guided by the ofttimes very inaccurate description of the woman herself. Nevertheless, small particles of chorionic tissue are usuallj readily recognized by the delicate coral-like character of the tissue. The decidua has usually a somewhat brownish color and is in layers. The ovum itself may vary in size from a small vesicle, half the size of the thumb, to a mass twice the size of the fist and laiger.

Microscopically, the diagnosis of a preceding pregnancy, and hence of an abortion, may be made from such spontaneously expelled material, or from the iarticles obtained by a uterine curette-ment. Susi)icion of a pi-egnancy may be aroused by the presence of proliferating glandular tissue as described in the chapter on jia-thology, and by the presence of decidua cells. Many have contended, and it seems to me with reason, that the positive diagnosis of an abortion can be made when large islands of typical decidua cells are found in the curetted particles. To those who liave examined many such specimens, the differentiation between such deciduous areas and those found in menstruation or in interstitial endometritis, is comparatively easy. If the number of decidua cells is few, and they are scattered, no i ositive conclusions can be drawn from their presence. A certain microscojiic diagnosis can of course be made by the iiuding of a single chorionic villus and typical proliferating syncytium, Such a picture can be produced by no other pathological condition and is of inestimable value in the testimony of cases of criminal abortion.

Fig. 19 shows such a villus with its characteristic epithelium. Where the fetus is not greatly macerated it will of course be readily recogtiized and the diagnosis rendered easy. Not infrequently, however, decomposition and partial liquefaction occur, so that the fetus becomes an indistinguishable jelly-like mass. In cases where the 5 5J? i:;;?;- v. A— . r:-.-.? H v h-. i

Figure 19 Normal placenta, sliowing the character of fetal epithelium, (v. Winckel.) tissues are too necrotic to take any cellular stain distinctly, we can at times obtain evidence by looking for traces of the eyes. The retinal pigment remains intact for months after fetal death, and may thus give evidence that the jelly-like mass is in reality a fetus. I recall an instance in which I was enabled to make the diagnosis of an abortion solely by tinding microsco jically such pigment spots in circular arrangement in the suspected fetal head.

Diagnosis of the Stage of Abortion. It is not enough, in a given case, merely to determine the fact that we are dealing with an abortion. We must further seek to determine in what stage the abortion may be, for the treatment is radically dependent upon this factor. In general, we speak of threatened abortion when symptoms have set in, but it is not yet too late to hope that the expulsion of the ovum may be prevented. Inevitable abortion is the term applied wlien-it is no longer possible to check the expulsion. Abortion is spoken of as incomplete when portions of the ovum are still left in the uterus. Complete aboi'tion refei's to the condition immediatclx alter the cxpnlsidii ol the oxuin has Ijcen entirely effected. Kecent abortion is the condition several days after complete exjiulsion of the ovum. Each of these five stages in the expulsive process luis distinctive signs and symptoms and must be carefully differentiated.

Threatened abortion is indicated by the occurrence of a vague sense of uneasiness, headache, backache, and frequently a marked increase in tlie desire to urinate. After these symptoms have persisted a day or so there is usually a show of blood in the vaginal discharge and a few abdominal cramps.

Inevitable abortion may be diagnosed: (1) When the amount of lihxxl lost is considerable or the bloody discharge prolonged for several weeks.

(2) When the pains become severe, occur at regular intervals, and are of a cramp-like character.

(3) When the cervix is dilated sufficiently to admit one finger.

(4) When in more developed pregnancies there has been a watery discharge indicative of a rupture of the membranes.

(5) When the fact of fetal death has been determined.

The diagnosis becomes more certain if several of these factors have been established. Boldt declares that if you have a persistent bloody grumous discharge, even without any marked x ains or cervical dilatation, an abortion is inevitable. The extent of cervical dilatation is of diagnostic value chiefly in primiparae. In women who have had children, there may be considerable cervical dilatation without any interruption of gestation. One of the questions that each one of us is often called upou to answer is: How long can I let this woman bleed before changing my diagnosis of threatened abortion to one of inevitable abortion? The question is not always easy to answer, for we must be guided by the total quantity of blood lost, the severity of uterine contractions, the methods of treatment previously employed, and by the patient's reaction to them. Whether the bleeding has lasted several weeks or not, abortion is not usually to be considered inevitable until the usual measures to check bleeding and expulsive pains have been tried in vain.

In general, vre may say that whexe treatment produces no decided effect within one week an abortion is likely to occur. Bleeding prolonged over three weeks is rarely attended by continuation of pregtiancy. A word of warning, however, should be given against using the watch and the calendar in the determination of this question. Our judgment must be based upon a consideration of all the various factors.

A sign of inevitable abortion emphasized by Tarnier is the effacement of the acute angle, formed anteriorly between the neck and body of the pregnant uterus. This effacement indicates a contraction of the longitudinal fibers of the uterus, and hence a descent of the ovum itself, owing to dislocation from its site of attachment.

Death of the fetus, when positively determined, makes abortion inevitable. It is not easy, however, to make a certain diagnosis of fetal death until a considerable period of time, usually months, has elapsed. By repeated examinations the fact can be determined that no enlargement of the uterus has taken place during this time, and death of the fetus can therefore be inferred. In some instances, upon the first examination, the anamnesis may point with certainty to a four or five months' pregnancy and the actual findings correspond to that of a one to two mouths' pregnancy. Hence, if symptoms indicative of abortion arise, and there is no special reason to suspect the honesty of the patient, the diagnosis of fetal death and retained inevitable abortion can be made, and the treatment instituted accordingly.

The diagnosis of incomplete abortion can be made by a consideration of the clinical course, an inspection of the pieces expelled, and a bimanual vaginal examination of the patient. Of the clinical signs the continuance of profuse bleeding, sometimes to the extent of hemorrhage, indicates that the uterus has not completely expelled its contents. There is normally after abortion a bloody discharge, but within twenty-four hours this changes to a slight bloody flow. On the other hand, where bits of placenta have been left, we have either a decided hemorrhage or the expulsion of numerous clots, usually rather dark in color. The pains of uterine contraction usually persist as long as material is still left in the uteius. These pains, however, are occasionally so feeble that the patient may be deceived into believing that everything has come away, when in reality a large piece of placenta is still retained.

Case No.-2. Irs. T. S., nnod 2G, was niarried in Januaiy, 1908, and since that time liad not nien. strnated. As slie did not wish to have a chihi she consulted a physician in March, and had him "open lut woiiili" witli an iiistruinciit. I'his was repeated several times and each tiiiic some clotted ll()(i(l was expelled. On April 27ih, she was referred to me under the iiiipix'ssion that she had miscarried, and that the continued pains and l)loody discharge were due to retained portions of the ovum. Upon examination, finding the cervix still closed and the uteius coriesponding in size to a 2 12 months' gestation, I put her to bed and gave her opiates in the hope that iregnancy might yet continue. On May 3d her pains suddenly became worse and on May-ith she miscarried. The placenta, however, was retained, so I packed the uterus and vagina with gauze. A large piece of placenta came away when the gauze was removed. Being a nullipara, and having a vagina unusually small, the digital exploration of the uterus was very difficult. Apparently there were only some shreds of decidua left. Three daj's later, however, continued bleeding and a temperature of 100.6 degrees induced me to examine her again, and this time I felt in the left cornua, still tightly adherent, a piece of placenta the size of a dollar. I was compelled to give an anesthetic to remove the piece from the uterus. The patient made a good recovery, her temperature went to normal and stayed there, and in two weeks I allowed her to get up. One month after the miscarriage, the menstruation returned and in spite of medicine persisted for two weeks. I therefore advised a curette-ment, but the patient refused to have it done. There was no fever or odor to the discharge, so that the diagnosis was clearly endometritis p o s t- a b 0 r t u m due to decidual Iemnants.

The inspection of the masses expelled must be carried out with the greatest care. If the ovum is apparently intact the only i oint to determine is whether or not the placenta corresponds in size to the duration of the pregnancy. This is a matter of considerable difficulty, even more so than after normal labor, for the variations in size of the placenta are very considerable, and its surface is always rough. One can also determine whether the decidua has come away with the ovum. The intact ovum of a pregnancy of the first month can be readily overlooked in the mass of bloodclots. It is seen as a glistening jelly-like mass one inch in diameter surrounded usually by a portiou of the moss-like chorionic villi (Fig. 20). Where the membranes have ruptured and the ovum has been expelled piecemeal, it happens not infrequently that only a i ortiou is saved for inspection. The statements of the patient, descriptive of such pieces, must be viewed critically, taking- into consideration the intelligence of the individual ou the one hand, and the accuracy of the description on the other. If the pieces have been saved, they had best be examined in normal salt solution. Fibrinous bloodclots must be

Figure 20 Ovum of four weeks, showing typical chorionic tufts. (Bryce.) dilterentiated from portions of decidua. The former are more readily crushed by the finger and more stringy. Pieces of chorion, when floating in water, will resemble sea-moss.

In many instances we can thus tell, by the history of the case, the character of material expelled, the cessation of pains and bleeding, that the abortion has been completed. It would only be increasing the risk of infection should we insist upon a digital examination. Where, however, doubt exists and it seems advisable to determine the question with greater certainty at once, we must proceed with vaginal bi-manual examination. The presence of numerous dark-colored bloodclots filling the vagina is suspicious of retained placenta. Coming to the cervix, we find this still dilated in incomplete abortion. The examining finger can, as a rule, make out the lower pole of. some object still in the uterus. This object maj be a bloodclot or a)ortion of the ovum. I loll has suggested the following luclluitl (if dirtciciitialing tiio Iwo: (a) During a iaiu caused by utciine contraction, tin- ovum, increased in size, smooth; ind tense, advances, while a bloodclot (h)cs not hcconic tense, nor does it advance.

(b) Tlie ovum presents a tense, resilient and convex surface, wliile the bloodclot is cone-shaped, apex downwaid, and non-elastic.

(c) If pressure is exerted on tiie fundus, in case the mass is an o uni, motion is luit triinsmitted to it as a whole, on account of its resiliency, while the bloodclot would be moved en masse, on account of its solidity.

"Where only pieces of placenta have been left in the uterus these can often be recognized at the external os by their rough surface and rather friable consistency. The cervix will be firmer to the touch than in tlie n-eguant state. This applies also to the fundus, which is somewhat reduced in size. During the first two months, however, it is a difficult matter to make out this diminution in size and increase in firmness. In abortion of the later months, however, it is rather easy and can positively establish the diagnosis of incomplete abortion. Firmness is here, as always, a relative term. The uterus of incomplete abortion is soft as comj ared with the uterus after complete abortion. Another characteristic of incomplete abortion is the sensation of crackling obtained on bi-manual compression of the uterus. This is due to the presence of foreign material in the uterine cavity. An intrauterine digital exploration for diagnostic purposes is occasionally necessary, but must always be made under the strictest aseptic precautions. The external genitals must be thoroughly cleaned and the hands of the accoucheur scrubbed as for an operation. If the examiner is accustomed to the use of rubber gloves, this additional safeguard against infection should be employed. In multiparae it is best to introduce the middle finger into the uterus. This procedure may be somewhat painful, but no anesthetic should be used unless preparations have been made for treating the case at once. If the ceivix is not sufficiently dilated to admit a finger, it is ordinarily inadvisable to dilate artificially unless the necessity for immediate diagnosis is urgent. Dilatation practically always requires narcosis. Its technique will be considered in detail under the head of treatment. The finger in the uterus can i-eadilv iiuikc out ill incdiuplt'ti ahortion a rough area ujioii wliiili larger or smaller pieces of tissue are still adherent, lu abortions of the third, fourth or fifth niontli, where the entire placenta is retained, the finger may enter the empty amniotic cavity and get everywhere the impression of a smootli surface. On closer pal iation, however, the placental site can be distinguished by its slightly raised nodular character.

The diagnosis of coinplctc abortion must be made from the same factors that have just been considered. The bleeding is scanty and the pains have ceased. The nterus is somewhat flatter than in the pregnant condition, and ni)ou bi-manual jiressure no blood-clot can be expelled from its cavity. The cervix is almost closed and the tissues have lost their former succuleiicy. In the breasts the free secretion of cholostrum is no longer present.

Recent abortion, that is to say, abortion that has occurred anywhere from two to fourteen days previously, occasionally demands diagnosis for medico-legal and therapeutic reasons. Especially where the suspicion of criminal aliortion is at hand a carefnl diagnosis is of the greatest importance. On digital examination we find, in abortions that have recently occurred, a rather free, usually blood-stained or brownish discharge, a patulous cervix and a somewhat enlarged uterus that is still a trifle softer than normal. From the microscopic examination of curetted)articles, or from the uterus at autopsy where death has occurred, we can determine the pieseuce of typical decidua or of chorionic villi. The nterus on gross inspection usually nesents a somewhat shaggy ayipearance at the site of the placenta.

Diagnosis of the Duration of the Pregnancy. It freijuently ha) pens that for diagnostic or medico-legal)urposes it is im mrtant to determine, as closely as possible, the duration of the pregnancy. This will in general prove easy if we keep in mind the anatomical characteristics of the three stages described in Chapter 3. The oecipito-sacral diameter of the fetus will show the monthly development according to the following rule: 1) to the iiftli mouth the length of the child in centimeters is equivalent to the S(uaie of the number of months it is old. Thus 1x1- 1 cm. 1st montli. 2xli 4 cms. 2d month. 3x3= 9 cms. 3d month. 4x4=l(J ems.-tth month. 5x5=25 cms. 5th month.

Diagnosis of the Cause of Abortion. Vvum tlic stainlihiiut of liidpli laxis (iiic (if tlic most iiiiportaiit tliin, i; s to (Ictcniiiiic is the OMUse of the aliortioii in n, i; i ('ii case, so tiiat, if jiossiiiu", measures may v adoplcd to iic cnt a recurrence of this mishai). According to Ciia. an (v. iiiciers llandliuch (hr Geburtshilfe) even tlie most careful investigation will not reveal the cause in the majority of cases.

Tile liisloiy of the case will often reveal the direct cause as some sort of exltrnal trauma (fall, etc.), or internal trauma (instrumental criminal abortion). The examination of the patient after abortion may h-ad to the discovery of a Ietroversion which may have been resihnsil)le for the lucuiature exjiulsion of the ovum. (Considerable iufonnatiou can also he obtained from a careful study of fetus and placenta. Should either show si)irocliaeta pallida or evidences of syphilitic changes, a positive diagnosis of the cause can be made. Thrombosis of the placenta, abnormalities of the cord, malformation of the fetus, will all indicate the direct cause.

Diagnosis of Criminal Abortion. It is often important from a medico legal standpoint to determine whether or not the abortion committed was criminal. In the living subject this can sometimes be determined by the presence of volsella jjunctures in the cervix. Such iunctures, howevei, usually disappear completely in two or three days. Grosser lesions about the vaginal vault and perforations caused by instruments are more readily recognizable. Postmortem, the diagnosis is not difficult if a perforation peritonitis has occurred. Tears and bruises in surrounding viscera are occasionally seen. The question of jn-egnancy must, however, be established with certainty in these cases, and here the microscopic examination by a competent pathologist of pieces excised from the uterus is of special importance. The value of this was demonstrated in the following case occurring in Missouri last year:

A minister and physician were implicated in the death of a young country girl, the accusation being that the minister had seduced her and that the physician had performed an abortion causing the death of the girl through sepsis. One of the claims made by the defense was that the girl was not pregnant and that therefore no abortion could have taken place. The uterus obtained at autopsy was examined by several lathologists. The answer was conclusive as soon as there were found, microscoj ically, a few tufts of chorionic villi still remaiuiug iu the uterine wall. Both miuister aud physician were sentenced to imprisonment. Such chorionic remnants can be found in every case of abortion if prolonged search be made, and too long a period has not elapsed between the examination and the abortion.

CHAPTER Vn

Differential Diagnosis In tlie differentinl diagnosis of abortion we must consider tlie possil)ility of one of the following five conditions: 1. Iitegular Menstruation of Functional Origin.

2. Hemorrhagic Endometritis.1. Snbmiuous Fibroid.
4. Carcinoma of the Uterus.
5. Ectopic Pregnancy.

1. Irregular Menstruation of Functional Origin. It is not at all uncommon to meet witli women who have spells of ameuorrlioea of three to four months' duration, which are followed b a free bloody discharge, with cramps and the passage of clots. To say in any one given instance that the case is not an abortion is not easy. The previous menstrual history, as well as the fact that on examination the uterus is of normal size and consistency, will usually clear the diagnosis. It is the amenorrhoea that leads to the assumption of a pregnancy, and later the patient is apt to interpret the sudden profuse return of menstruation as the onset of an abortion. The liquid character of menstrual blood is of considerable diagnostic value. Frequently, we are called upon several weeks or even months after such a bloody discharge from the uterus to decide whether or not it was an abortion. Where we have only the patient's statements to guide us it is impossible to give a positive answer.

2. Hemorrhagic Endometritis is characterized by irregular bleeding attended with uteiiue pains, by an enlarged, somewhat softened, uterus, and occasionally by the expixlsion of pieces from the uterus (membranous form, dysiiicnorrhoca membranacca). From this description it will be evident that a differentiation from abortion will not always be easy or even possible. In fact, in certain cases of membranous dysmenorrhoea only the microscopic examination of the pieces expelled will settle the diagnosis. In general, however, the following points will serve to distinguish these two conditions:

Endometritis.
1. Menstruation too frequent.
2. Pains worst at onset of I eriod.

3. Tendency to clot slight, blood dark in color.
4. Uterus a little larger and softer.
5. Microscopically pieces show glandular or connective tissue hyperplasia.
1. Usually some amenorrhoea before bleeding starts.
2. Pains slight at onset, in- creasing in severity.?. Blood in large clots, often bright red.
4. Uterus markedly increased in size and softness.
5. Microscopically decidua and chorion jiresent in pieces expelled.

Case No. 3. Mrs. A. P., aged 40, had her last child three years previously, and had been regular in her menstruation up to December, 1908. In January she went over her time two weeks and then began to bleed persistently. Larger and smaller clots were passed,)ut no pieces that resembled an ovum. The uterus was enlarged to the size of an orange, and soft. After a week's rest without imin-ovement a curettement was decided upon. The probability of an abortion was much lessened by the continued absence of fever and of any odor to the discharge. The curettement showed the cavity of the uterus about 4 12 inches deep. Microscopic examination of the curetted particles revealed merely chronic inflammatory changes of the mucosa without any evidence of a previous pregnancy. The diag-nosis was therefoie chronic endometritis and metritis with beginning menopause.

3. Fibroid Tumors, especially of the submucous type, may cause the uterus to ai)pear softer and more spherical, but here there is apt to be a history of profuse and too frequent menstruation. The value of a good clinical history becomes evident, since the physical findings may permit of no differentiation. As a rule, however, careful palpation will show in cases of fibroid tumors some irregularity of outline and consistency. In more advanced cases of abortion (third to fifth month), the similarity between them and submucous fibroids IIfkVl-. XIKlx AND TlikAI'MKXT Ol AliolflloN.

ill process of eximlsidii into the vagina must l)e kept in iiiiiiid. Both may give rise to iroiuse liemorrhage and an odorous discharge of necrotic material. The liistoiv of ainciionlioea, increased softness

Figure 21 F"ibroid polyp of uterus, giving rise at times to symptoms resfmhliiig an abortion (Montgomery).

of the pregnant uterus, greater friability of placental tissue over iibroid tissue, reiiler the differentiation comparatively simple.

4. Cancer of the Uterus must likewise be distinguished from abortions. If the cancer be located in the cervix this will not be

Figure 22 Beginning cancer of tlie cervix (Case 4). clinically resembling an abortion. I'terus rtmovni by Wertheim's radical hysterectomy.

difficult, but if it be located in the body of the uterus the differentiation will have to be based, to a considerable extent, on the i)atient's history. Cancer of this type rarely appears at an age when child-bearing is likely to occur, but when it does, the continuous bloody discharge with passage of clots and necrotic shreds may closely simulate an abortion. Here the microscope is necessary to clear up the nature of the trouble. We must remember, however, that a form of malignant tvmior of the uterus, called chor io-epi t helioma, from the fact that it develops from the chorionic epithelium, occasionally develops after an abortion. This tumor can be differentiated from cancer liy the character of the tumor tissue (resembling placenta), and by the frequency of metasta. ses (vagina, lungs and brain).

Case No. 4. Illustrative of the differeutial diagnosis from cancer of the uterus, the following history is of interest: Mrs. B., aged.36, had had three children, "the last one six years previously. Since this childbirth there had been some abdominal pains. Her menstruation had usually been only slightly irregular. In April, 1! I0S, she had felt nauseated. Thought she felt a quivering in the abdomen in August. On August 1, at the time of her period, there was so free a hemorrhage for two days, that it necessitated her going to bed and sending for a doctor. The bleeding lasted five days. The patient thought she was probably having a miscarriage. Her physician found a cervix suspicious of malignancy. He referred her to me on August 15,1908. T found a uterus larger and softer than normal and a cervix that l)led very readily on touching. The possibility of a retained abortion of several weeks' development could not be positively excluded, but the cervix looked so i-agged that a piece was removed for microscopic examination. Tiiis showed a typical beginning carcinoma. Consequently, I performed a panhysterectomy. The body of the uterus on section presented a markedly thickened endometrium, but no trace of any previous pregnancy. Her nausea and quivering were evidently due to otlier causes. The recovery from the operation was uneventful.

5. Tubal Pregnancy. ost difficult is the differentiation between tubal pregnancy, or, rather, tubal abortion, and intrauterine abortion, especially when the latter is associated with inflannnatory I; K I-XTIOX AND IlikATMENT OF Al-olilloX.

hoiihlo of the adnoxa. It is a very common event. o liave a uterus curetted on flie. su)i)ositioii that tliere is a post-abortive i-etention of placenta, only to discover a little later that the correct diagnosis was extra-uterine)re! inan(y. I'o keep from niakini;-sncli mistakes we must bear the followini;:)oints in mind: In the histoiy of tlie ease we are a it to have in uterine al)irtion a longer period of complete amenorrhoea before bleeding starts. Tubal

Amnion

Uterine cavity

Partially separated placenta.

Figure 23 Tubal pregnancy. In this case the ovum became imbedded in the interstitial portion of the tube, thus making the differentiation from normal gestation even more difficult (Bumm).

abortion is more apt to occur between the fourth and sixth week, whereas uterine abortion occurs with greatest frequency between the eighth and twelfth week. In tubal abortion the onset of pains and bleeding is often attended by dizziness or even fainting, owing to the shock of intra-abdominal hemorrhage. Furthermore, the cramps or labor pains are felt on the attected side, whereas in uterine abortion the cramps are directly in the hypogastrium. omiting, due to peri- toneal irritation, is more often found in tubal gestation. The character of the bleeding is of some differential value. In tubal abortion, for instance, where only decidual tissue is expelled from the uterus, the amount of bleeding is not severe and often there is only a prolonged brownish discharge. In uterine abortions, on the other hand, there are apt to be many clots, a copious bleeding, and pieces of placental tissue expelled. Again, in tubal abortion bimanual examination reveals a slightly enlarged uterus with a one-sided oval or sausage-shaped mass, the size of a fist or even larger, very sensitive to pressure, rather boggy to the touch, semi-fluctuating, adherent; whereas in uterine abortion we have a spherical, large uterus, not sensitive, with perhaps a one-sided or double-sided mass of variable size depending on the amount of associated inflammatory trouble in the adnexa. If this inflammatory mass is sensitive, there are apt to be several degrees of fever, 101 to 103, whereas it is the rule in tubal abortion for the thermometer to register only 99.5 to 100. The pulse, on the other hand, is more often rapid in the latter condition, ranging between 100-130 in accordance with the extent of the internal hemorrhage. The differential diagnosis will occasionally be impossible until the patient has been under observation for some time. Another trying element in the management of these cases is the unwillingness of the patient to be confined to her bed or go to a hospital for observation. Wishing something done at once, she often hurries the physician into measures whose consequences are fatal to the patient. Many cases are thus on record where a liuvry-up diagnosis of retained placenta was made and the uterus emjitied digitally or with a curette, only to have the patient collapse immediately afterwards, and die before she could be taken to the liosiiital and be operated on. Try your utmost, therefore, to have these doubtful cases go to the hospital, where they can be closely studied, and where in an emergency everything is at hand for operation. In the course of a week or two it will become evident either by the character of material expelled or by the increase in size of the affected tube whether the abortion is uterine or tubal.

Case No. 5. A good illustiation of the difficulty in differential diagnosis between abortion and tubal pregnancy is given by the following history: Mrs. S., a woman of 39 years, had had two children, the last one six years ago. On July 11, 1906, I was called to her residence iiiul Joiuul her sunvrin. i; witli severe craiii! like jiniiis in the lel't side.-Her teini)eriture was KM degrees and hci- pulse fiom 100 to 120. Slie h)oked rather ialc. Tiitil June 4tli, her menstruation had always l)een reguhir. In the month of July there was no flow until the Stli, one week over her time. Then a slight bloody discharge began, which was still presimit on-July 11th, when 1 lii'st saw her. There was some dizziness and nausea, hut no vomiting.

On examination I found a uterus slightly larger than normal and somewhat softer. To the left side was a tender, sausage-shaped mass, extending from the uterine horn to the eul-de-sac. This mass was only slightly niovalile.

The likelihood of a tubal pregnancy was not to be denied, so the l)atieut was takeji to lullan ihy Jlosjiital and kept under observation. The pains rapidly subsided and the bleeding gradually slackened under continvied rest in bed and sedatives. The temperature and pulse returned to normal on the third day. On leaving the hospital two weeks later, the swelling on the left side had almost disa)peared, but the uterus still felt unusually large and soft. It was only then that the diagnosis was changed from extra-uterine gestation to intrauterine gestation with threatened abortion. The patient remained well until October, when she very suddenly miscarried, the fetus showing a development of four and one-half months.

The material expelled should be saved, and, if not too decomposed, sectioned microscopically. A diagnostic curettage can, if necessary, be made without an anesthetic and sufficient material obtained for microscopic study. In fact, such a procedure, with due care to asepsis and uterine perforation, presents no special difficulty. The presence of chorionic villi or epithelium is proof of an intra-uter-ine pregnancy, whereas, if decidua alone is found on examining many sections, it is very suspicious of tubal pregnancy. In this connection we must remember that there are now on record in the neighborhood of one hundred cases of combined extra-uterine and intrauterine pregnanej Hence the possibility of such an event, in spite of its rarity, must be kei)t in mind in making a diagnosis.

To summarize ouce more the differentiation between tubal abortion and uterine abortion we have: 1. Occurs most often between 4th and Gth week.

2. Pains severe, one-sided, at- tended with faintness and at times vomiting.

3. Bleeding moderate, brown- ish,. stringy, decidua at times expelled.

i. Bimanually, uterus only slightly enlarged.

5. Bimanually, a mass to one side, semi-fiuctuating, sensitive, often sausage-shaped, boggy to the touch.

6. Temperature 99.5 to 100.

7. Pulse 110 to 1.30.

8. Pieces from uterus show only decidua microscopically.

Uterine Abortion.

1. Most frequent between 8th and 12th week.

2. Pains moderate, central.

3. Bleeding copious, reddish, clotted, x lacental pieces expelled, necrotic odor.

4. Bimanually, uterus enlarged in accordance with stage of pregnancy.

5. Bimanually, either normal tubes and ovaries, or, if associated with tubal infection, usually a double-sided mass, also sensitive to touch and semi-fluctuating.

6. Temperature (if tul il in- fection) 102 to 103.

7. Pulse 90 to 100.

8. Pieces from uterus show chorionic villi or s lcy-tium with decidua microscopically.

Prognosis In his excoutiil little iiiouugiaph on "xlbortions," T. Gaillard Thomas relates: "A day or two ago I consulted a certain author in regard to the prognosis of abortion and I found that he pictured it in a very rose-colored way, stating that there was but little danger of a fatal issue and that the morbidity was small. The facts of the case I believe to be directly the opposite of this. There can be no question whatever that a large number of deaths occur which are directly or indirectlj due to abortion, but which are set down to other causes" (p. 12).

The prognosis of abortion will depend on many factors; on whether it was spontaneous or artificial, whether it was complete or incomplete, whether operative measures were necessary, whether all procedures were carried out with strict asepsis, whether the patient was given the necessary bed-rest afterwards, etc., etc. In general, we find that the mortality after abortions is greater than after full-terai pregnancies. Rimette observed 27 deaths in 1,437 abortions (about 2 per cent.). Treub in 202 criminal ajjortions recoided 9 deaths (4.5 per cent.) and 38 seriously ill (19 per cent.). These figures are considerably above the figures of confinement cases. The main reason of this more serious prognosis is the danger of infection and the greater frequency of operative interference. Thus, out of Rimette's 1,437 cases, only 627 were spontaneous; the balance were either infected or complicated cases. Few women fully appreciate these facts. Upon inquiry the majority will say they thought a miscarriage was a simple thing, much less dangerous than having a baby. In fact, many who would otherwise not think it worth while to check a beginning miscarriage can be induced to follow directions, after the correct prognosis, as compared with child-birth, has been explained to them.

In spontaneous, complete abortions there is hardly ever any trouble afterwards. In fact, instances are recorded where women after such au abortion have continued with their work and never experienced any bad ettects from it. Where there is some complication, however, the prognosis becomes more clouded. The danger of bleeding in abortion comes usually not from one severe hemorrhage, but from long-continued bleeding in a moderate degree. It is only on rare occasions that there is a sudden gush of blood, with fainting and collapse, and, where this happens, the syncope itself tends to check the bleeding. "Wliere death results from hemorrhage in abortion, we usually get the following historj: After persistent, rather free bleeding for a week or two, with no opportunity for the patient to recuperate, digital or instrumental removal of the placenta becomes necessary; the shock and additional bleeding of this procedure so depleting her strength that the outcome is fatal.

Another complication that incieases the immediate and remote dangers of abortion is septic infection. The subject will be considered more in detail later on. Here it need only be stated that while there was only one death out of 267 cases which were free of fever in Sittner's clinic, his 35 septic cases resulted in 3 fatalities. Maygrier's figures are even more striking, for, while the mortality of his spontaneous abortions was but 0.57 per cent., that of the criminal aliortions was 56. S per cent. The hitter figures are higher than most obstetricians have found. Siich an infection, even if it does not actually cause the death of the individual, may lead to pelvic abscess, laarametritis, chronic pelvic ideritonitis, metritis, salpingitis, ovarian abscess, etc., depending upon the original site and course of the iufiammatory process. The prognosis becomes much graver so soon as the infectious germs have gone beyond the limits of the uterus.

Retained i lacenta makes the prognosis more serious, in so far as it necessitates some form of operative treatment. The dangers from such operative interference are four-fold: (1) The danger of infection from the instruments, the hands of the operator, the genitals of the patient, or from the spreading of germs already introduced by jirevious manipulations upon areas more sensitive to infection.

(2) The danger of severe hemorrhage through the loosening of an adherent bit of placenta, the relaxation of an atonic uterus, or through cervical tears.

(JO PKKVKXrioX I Ilil. AI. MKXI OF ABOHTION.

(o) I'lie (l; iiii; cr ol pcrruratidU in (.-areless iiistiunieutauou or in very soft uterine wall.

(4) TJie danger of ceivical huaration, with its resultant increased tendency to infection and endocervicitis.

Finally, tlic piognosis of aliniiiiin Ixh-onies less favorable when the after-treatment has imt ixcn carefnlly looked aftei. Usually a rallum cxtondod rosi in Itcil is necessary, approximately two weeks, with special attention to the re-establishing of good geneial health. The anemia resulting from loss of blood or infection nnist be corrected, or nervous and digestive distui-banccs will result. Particularly in women who have had several abortions in rapid succession, we find that the nervous system has been seriously undcrmiikMl, often leaving them in a semi-invalid condition.

Prophylaxis Before Conception

AVIieu we cousider how often it liapjiens that the onl- pregnancy early in marital life results in a miscarriage, or tliat there are re-lieated miscairiages, and that at each such event the life of a human being is wasted just as traly as if it had attained adult life, then the l)revention of this accident assumes its true importance in the development of the race. Thousands of male spermatozoa and hundreds of female ova m; iy be spared from the economy of the universe, but each fertilized ovum implanted in the uterine mucosa is a precious object, that we must, by every effort in our power, save from premature destruction. Only too often it is a race between the spermatozoon and the gonococcus to see which will iirst reach the Fallopia7i tube and there cause either fertilization of the ovum or infection of the mucosa. Only too often do we find that an abortion, either spontaneous or iirovoked, gives the opi)Oi'tunity for a localized gonorrhoea to spread to the tubes, and by the resulting inflammation effectively precludes the)ossibility of any subsequent concei)tion. All these considerations make us feel that we must guard zealously each ovum, and that the many problems in the pievention of miscarriage demand the most careful study.

Naturally our prophjdaxis will depend ujion whether or not conception has already taken)lace, upon whether or not abortion is already threatened. I have therefore subdivided the STibject into

A. Prophylaxis before conception.

B. P r o i h 1 a X i s during p i r e g n a n c y.

C Prevention of threatened abortion. 1). Prevention of criminal abortion.

Ill the present chapter cousideration will ho liiiiiitcd to measures ciiiiiliiyihl before conception. Only by a coi-ixct appreciation of the cause of prccccling abortions in a. iven case can we airive at a satisfactory conclusion as to what should be done to j revent occurrences in the future. Some of the causes are, one might say, acute, and some chronic. Tlius some come on in otherwise healtliy motliers so suddenly (sexcrc lall. infcclious fever) as almost to preclude the possibility of cniplon ing any)reventive measures before or during pregnancy.

Where, however, tlie miscaniage has been due to some avoidable cause, we can at times do much to prevent a recurrence. And here let nic first of all speak of recurrent or "habitual" ab(U'tion, as it is usually termed. In many of these patients the frequent abortions are due primarily to an increased irritability of the uterus. It is well known that a patient who has once aborted is more likely to have the accident happen a second time, particularly if a second pregnancy follows quickl upon the first. Prophylaxis in these cases consists in enjoining on the patient an interval of from eight to nine months before another pregnane is permitted. For obvious reasons this is not always practicable, but we must at least warn our patients of the dangers, if these precautions are not observed.

Under the head of diseases which predispose to placental thrombosis, and hence to abortion, we mentioned endometritis. The term is a broad one and here refers more particulaily to the glandular hyperplastic form of endometritis. "Where we find such a disease we must first employ the conservative methods of treatment (hot douches, tampons, ergot, rest) and if this prove ineffective as shown by continued backache, menorrhagia, dysmenorrhoea or leucorrhoea, a thorough curettement should be done before conception again ensues.

Cervical tears are not as often responsible for abortion as some writers would have us believe. It takes a pretty large tear to be responsible for an abortion. More frequently a tear is only one of a number of factors. Where other methods of prophylaxis have proved a failure, or where the cervical tear extends out to the paia-metrium, a repair of the cervix (trachelorrhaphy) should be done.

Where the uterus is retroverted, it does not by any means follow that a pregnancy cannot go to term. In a large percentage of cases the uterus will, without any assistance, gradually assume its correct position. But since we can never tell whether tlie case in point will be fortunate enough thus to accommodate itself to circumstances, it is best, when we have a patient with retroverted uterus who has previously had an abortion, to try to correct the position before the next pregnancy ensues. This is not always 230ssible. A uterus may be so adherent that it will resist the most persistent efforts to free it and bring it foiward, and yet, through the increased softening and succu- tjssab ":

Figure 2A Introducing the pessary (step one). The pessary is slipped up to the cervix and the vaginal linger passed over the upper bi-im (Crossen).

lence of the tissues because of pregnancy, such a uterus may correct itself spontaneously, or by slight pressure be brought forward. Our attitude before conception, however, must be to treat a retroverted uterus as a possible factor m producing abortion; hence it is better to keep the uterus in a correct position by means of a pessary. The manner of introducing such a pessary is shown in Figures 24 and 25.

PREVENTION AMI lltl. A IM I. XI Ol A li( )lill()N.

When oitlut ol the pjirciils is in a iiiaikcdiy aiiomic condition or tiuir liviuial licalIli iu any way seriously jiffectcil we must guard agiiinst the possibility ol a iii', iiiaiiiy. (on((')tioii is less likely to take plaoe at sudi tiiiics, hut wiieii it does occur it not int"re((uontly results in an ovum with diminisiied vitality, resulting in Ietal death. In such instances a jirolonged vacation, or the administration of iron toiiii iic iaralioiis, sucli as Ijli. xir Iron, ( )uiiiinc, anl Slivcjininc, in

Figure 25 Intioducing the pessary (step two). The vaginal Hnger depresses the brim of the pessary till it can lie slipped beneath the cervix and finally lies in the posterior vaginal fornix. (Crossen.) teaspooniul doses three times a day for many weeks, together with suitable hygiene as to food and exercise, will result in the desired improvement. We must use our judgment as to when it is safe to permit a renewed gestation. When such a building up of the general nutrition has taken place pregnancy will usually no longer be interrupted.

Many writers sug-gest that whenever yon are in doubt as to the cause of a previous abortion you should jiut tlie patient on anti-syphilitic treatment. Mercury and potassium iodide given in moderate amounts will often yield surprising results. If conception is not)ermitted until two years after the onset of the disease, and during this time the patient is)ut on a thorough course of anti-sj-pliilitic treatment, the probability is that no miscarriage will ensue.

The treatment that is now recognized as the quickest and most reliable is the hypodermic injection of either the bichloride or some other related salt of mercury. Injections should be made daily.

The AVassermann blood-serum reaction is a test of unquestioned value in the diagnosis of latent syphilis, and is therefore of great importance in determining the cause of an abortion. Since the reaction disappears with the cure of the disease, it is also of inestimable value in the prevention of abortion. In other words, if we can tell just at what time an individual is rid of her syphilitic infection, we can indicate when conception will be carried to full-term and result in the birth of a healthy, living child.

The reaction is. however, somewhat complicated and must for the iresent be limited to the laboratory of the trained pathologist. The principle upon which it is based is that of hemolysis, or the solution of red-blood cells under certain conditions. In order for the blood cells to be dissolved, a certain substance known as complement is necessary to complete the reaction. In other words, we must have the red cells, the h e m o l y s i n, or dissolving agent, and the complement, which is, so to speak, the match that sets oft" the reaction. A similar reaction takes place between bacteria and the substance known as bacteriolysin, by which the bacteria are dissolved. In the specific instance of syphilis, the sjjiro-chaete pallida are dissolved by the syphilitic lysin. In a person infected with syphilis, considerable quantities of this lysin are formed and are found in the blood-serum. There is normally present in the blood-serum of every individual a certain quantity of complement, or. to repeat our comparison, a certain number of matches. This complement is destroyed when the serum is heated to 56 C. For the imrpose of this reaction we must know the exact quantity of complement in a given case. Hence, this must be added separately.

The test. is therefore as Idudw-s: Tlie serum of the suspected individual is taken and Inalcd to 5()" C to destroy the contained complement. Then there is added to a definite quantity of serum, a definite (uantity nl complement, and a definite quantity of spirochaete pailiila or llieir equivalent substance, called antigen. Placed in an incubator for one hour, the bacteriolytic action takes jilace, piovided tlir leisdn was spliilitic. Thereby, however, all the ((ini ilen: ent is consumetl. J'lie niatclies are, so to speak, all burnt out, so tluit wlien we now add red cells and hemolysin nothing-is left to set off the reaction by which the red cells are dissolved. T f the red cells collect at the bottom of the test-tube undissolved, the complement has been used up and the patient therefore has sy j) li i I i s. Several control tests must always be made so as to see that all substances used are working properly. If carefully performed, the test is now shown to be a fairly certain way of determining the presence or absence of syphilis. As in every laboratory test, there are sources of error, but these are very few in the hands of the skilled pathologist. In every large city in America there can be found two or more persons qualified to do this reaction. This test is rather a costly procedure, so that for the present its general usefulness will have to be restricted, but doubtless with time, this y)ractical disadvantage will also disappear.

Prophylaxis During Pregnancy

General Measures. In reviewing tlie causes of abortion it was seen that in many instances the exciting factor was some breach of liygiene. It is well, therefore, for the pregnant woman to be careful in her way of living, particularly during those early months of pregnancy when the uterus is most sensitive to irritation. Such precautions are ijarticularly to be observed when an abortion has previously occurred.

Travel, especially in a railroad train, is very apt to stir up uterine contractions. Horseback riding or any form of exercise or locomotion which causes much jolting or jarring of the body is bound to be harmful.

Case Xo. 6. In illustration of what some women can endure without interruption of pregnancy, the following history is of interest. The patient was a woman of twenty-four years, who had had two children, the last one being born three years ago. She came of a family of German circus performers and both she and her husband were trapeze g7T3masts. They crossed the ocean to fill a contract with Ringiing's circus, but soon afterwards the woman became pregnant. While in New York, in March, there was some irregular bleeding for two days. At this time she must have been pregnant about two months. She continued at her strenuous em-plo iuent. Throughout April there was almost continuous bleeding and occasional pains in the lower abdomen. Xevertheless, owing to her contract, she did not dare fail to make her appearance, and continued her nightly trapeze performance. On April 29th, when on the advice of her Chicago physician she consulted me, I found pregnancy had advanced in spite of the bleeding and a partial dilatation of the cervix. Bleeding was very free. I advised absolute rest. During her week's stay in St. Louis she did not miscarry. Her subsequent history I could not learn.

The use. ol tlio sewing luachiue sliuiild be jn-uhibited whenever there is any tendency to miscnrriage. Experience has shown tliat this form of work i)redisposes to an interruption of iireunaiicy. Those mild forms of trauma tliat are applied directly to the uterus are even more likely to start an abortion. One of the most imiior-tant is constipation, which promotes uterine contractions in two ways; (1) it incieases pelvic congestion; (2) it causes by the straining at stool a loosening of the placental attachment or a hemorrhage into the decidua. Coitus, wliich may be permitted with certain limitations during pregnancy, must be absolutely piohibited wherever there is a tendency to miscarry. It should be done at rare intervals and without deej)jienetration. The importance of observing this rule cannot be too strongly insisted upon. Here too, we have a combination of congestion ami trauma wliidi only too often leads to the termination of the pregnancy.

It is well known that after conception has taken place, and the menses have ceased to ajipeai. tiiere occur more or less well-defined menstrual waves at about the time of the expected flow. During this period we have a raised blood-pressure, often some backache, and a greater tendency to nervous irritability. At such times women are more apt to miscarry and for this reason they must keep doubly quiet. Thomas advises keeping patients, who have irevi-ously aborted, and who are very anxious to avoid another mishap, in bed for twelve days during this menstrual period: four days before, four days during, four days after the expected time. Where the interval between menstrual)eriods is irregular, it becomes more difficult to figure out just when to observe this rest. It will ordinarily be impossible to insist upon such a twelve days' rest in bed, except in cases of habitual abortion where ordinary measures have failed, but in every case special care should be taken at the time of the menstrual wave to refrain from doing anything that might prove a source of irritation.

Syphilis. Where we are certain that syphilis has caused the abortion or where we have reason to suspect such an etiological factor, a vigorous course of anti-syphilitic treatment should be instituted. Where preg-nancy has ensued before the discovery of the disease we must get our patient under the influence of mercury as rapidly as possible. Inunctions, injections, the iodides or the mixed treatment not only do not interfere with the progress of pregnancy, but lessen the danger to the fetus and distinctly reduce the frequency of premature labor.

Other Causes. If the mother is generally run down, if she is in what may be termed the pre-tubercular condition, she is apt to miscarry unless every effort is made to restore her strength. Taylor thinks this "strumous" group of cases almost as numerous as the syphilitic abortions. In his opinion a case would belong to this group if it presents the following characteristics: (1) Indications of low vitality in mother or father or both; (2) a "strumous" family history; (3) remarkable result of an essentially anti-strumous treatment carried on for a long time. This anti-strumous treatment consists of Syrupus Ferri Phosphati Compositus, teaspoouful three times a day, and Cod Liver Oil, teaspoonfnl to tablesiioonfnl three times a day.

Where there is cardiac incompetency, due to a valvular heart disease or some other cause, the increased congestion of the genital tract is apt to cause contractions unless quickly remedied. Digitalis, strychnine or strophanthus must be emi)loyed. depending on the special indications. In the same way, if the functions of the kidneys are interfered with, dietary and medicinal measures must be employed. The presence of allnmiiuuria or oedema necessitates active eliminative treatment.

The various infectious diseases that occasionally give rise to abortions usually run a definite course, and ail that we can hope to do, for the most part, is to promote the excretion of toxic material from the maternal system, and by cold sponging to reduce the fever if it should be so high as to endanger the child's life through hyperpyrexia, or hasten uterine contractions on the part of the mother.

In smallpox it is important to re-vaccinate at once in order to diminish the. severity of the infection and to reduce the danger to the fetus.

Special conditions about the uterus are often noticed for the first time after preg-nancy has begun. Adhesions to one side or the other may interfere with the normal uniform enlargement of the organs. Such adhesions may usually be readily broken nji by massage, since the increased hyperemia during pregnancy makes them more pliable.

Every now and then it becomes imperative to resort to operative measures for the relief of appendicitis, gallstones, ovarian cysts, etc., IHKVKXTIOX AXl) TKF. AT. M KXl dl A li(l; TIOX.

ill tlu course of; i)n, i ii; iiicy. Wliciicvcr sucli iiic. isuics arc cin-liloycd, special care is necessary to avoid an alkntioii. If considerable doses of opiates in liypodennic lorni are injected, uterine contractions can usually be avoided and the jnennancy go on to Iull term. In tliis connection, it is well to remember tiiat vaginal operations or opei-ations upon the external genitals are more apt to cause a disturbance oi jtregnanc- tlian a hipaiotoniy, pi-ovided the latter is not attended by inncli shock.

Whether Ilom adhesions, or from a relaxation of its ligaments, the pregnant uterus often lies in a r e t r o v e r t e d or r e t r o f l e x e d

Figure 26 The knee-chest posture. The knees should be separated about one foot; the thighs perpendicular; the breasts resting upon the table; the face turned to one side. (Crossen.) position. Sometimes such a malposition may correct itself spontaneously, Ijut it is best not to leave this to chance, for, if uncorrected, the most serious complications, incarceration Yith almost certain abortion, will result. Hence, in every case of retroverted pregnant uterus, we must seek to correct the faulty position as soon as possible. The method to be employed will always have to be a gentle one to avoid any undue stimulation of uterine contractions.

The forcible elevation of the uterus under anesthesia must, therefore, be a last resort. The first measure to be employed and one usually successful in the early months is the frequent assumption of the knee-chest position by the patient. All clothing around the waist must be loosened and the position assimied for five to ten minutes two to three times a day. (Fig. 26.) Should this fail to bring the laterus forward with the addition of gentle bi-manual manipulation we can resort to the mercury pressure treatment. This con-

Figure 27 Instruments for the pressure-weight treatment. The rubber bag. or colpeu-rynter. is caught with the dressing forceps and after lubrication is introduced into the vagina. Then tlie funnel is attached to the bag and from one to two pounds of liquid mercury poured from the bottle into the bag. The tube of the bag can then be tied or clamped. The bag must of course be sterilized before introduction.

sists of filling an ordinary colpeurynter or rubber dilating bag with from one to two fluid ounces of mercury, after it has previously been IDlaced as high in the vagina as conditions will permit. The hips of the patient are then raised so that she is in a moderate Trendelenburg position. After fifteen to twenty minutes an examination is made to see if the pressure of the mercury has been sufficient to correct the malposition. The treatment can be repeated on the following daj if unsuccessful. This gradual stretching of adhesive bands is preferable to anj rougher measures. After its position has been corrected, the uterus must be kept in puice by a i)roperly fitting pessary. The Albert Smith pessary will usually be found most serviceable. Great cai e must be taken not to use too large a ring, as pressure irritation and necrosis are more likely to result in the oedematous vaginal wall of the pregnant woman than at other times. Such patients should report to us every week or two to guard against this, and to see Ihnt tlie pessary fulfills its function of holding the

Figure 28 Retroverted pregnant uterus, being brought forward by a combination of the knee-chest position together with manual pressure The cervix is caught witli the volsellum and pulled toward the vaginal outlet while the vaginal fingers press the fundus upward out of the pelvis. (Bumm.) uterus forward. After the fourth month the uterus rises above the brim of the pelvis, and the pessary can be safely removed;

in fact, it is better to do so, for at times even such a small foreign object as the pessary in the vagina may give rise to premature uterine eon-tractions.

Cause Unknown. Where the etiological factor in the previous abortions cannot be ascertained, we can employ, beside the general measures already referred to, certain medicines calculated to diminish uterine irritability. Viburnum has long been recommended for this purpose, but its powers do not seem to be very active. Half a teaspoonful of the Fluid Extract may be given three times daily. Asafoetida in two-grain gelatin-coated pills, two to six pills daily, has met with success in some cases. Lomer, in cases of doubtful etiology, gives i otassium iodide in combination with iron.

Habitual Abortion. In some women the tendency to abort is so strong that extreme measures must be resorted to. At times a miscarriage has been averted only by keeping the patient in bed from the sixth week of pregnancy to the fifth month. That such a prolonged rest is apt to be to some extent debilitating nmst be admitted, hence we must seek by mild gymnastics and massage, by fresh air and good food, to keep the patient in as good general condition as possible. Particiilar care as to regulation of the bowels must here be observed, since otherwise constipation is certain to result, with consequent increased liability to abortion.

Case No. 7. Mrs. F., aged 26, married one and one-half years; had had one miscarriage five months after her marriage, in spite of the fact that at the very onset of bleeding every precaution such as rest in bed, sedatives, etc., was observed. A period of two months elapsed from the time of the first show of blood until the ovum was finally expelled. The placenta was retained and had to be removed digitally. The recovery was perfectly normal. There were no untoward symptoms after this first miscarriage.

Just about one year later pregnancy again set in, the last men-stiuation occurring on September 20, 1908, and being of the usual duration. During October there was morning sickness and toward the end of the month a few slight cramps. She was kept in bed at this time for one week, and told to abstain from every occupation that would in any way be a source of strain or excitement to her. She was practically indoors all montli. In spite of these precautions, the patient made a few extra preparations for a Thanksgiving dinner on November 26th, and on that afternoon was seized with cranii3-like pain in the lower abdomen. She went to bed at once and was given opiates in large doses, but nevertheless on tlio following day expelled a fresh ovum of about six or seven weeks' development. The ilacenta and fetus came away together, and the decidua, after packing the iiteriue cavity with gauze (Figures 11-12), was expelled two days later. The subseciuent course of the case was uneventful. The temperature never rose over 100 degrees.

As the couple were anxious to have a child, I performed a thorough curettement two weeks after Uic miscarriage, and found in the uterine mucosa evidences of endometritis. A luetic history is not obtainable, nor did the microscopic examination of the placenta reveal any evidences of lues. During the next pregnancy I shall order the patient confined to bed, or at least to her bedroom, during the first four months of gestation.

Prevention of Threatened Abortion

The term "threatened abortion" is a little ambiguous. What is meant is that the opening steps of an abortion, . e., the uterine contractions and partial loosening of the placental attachment of the ovum have taken place, but that they have not yet reached the stage at which retreat is impossible. The ovum may still go to full-term larovided the expulsive process is checked. How difficult it is to say just when this stage has been reached has already been emphasized. Whenever doubt exists we must assume that the expulsion is not inevitable and set our therapeutic indications accordingly.

Although we have no definite statistics on the subject, the probability of checking a beginning abortion does not seem to be very great. The jdroportion of failures among the lower classes is nearly 9 out of 10 owing to the fact that most women absolutely refuse to carry out instructions to the full extent. They do not see the necessity of remaining in bed a long time, and in many instances are rather anxious to liave the abortion take place. But even when this is not the case, and where financial circumstances will permit the individual to take absolute rest for a long period, the results are none too good.

Here the physician will only too often find a conflict between duty and self-interest. Many a patient has discharged her doctor because he has kept her in bed a long time, uselessly, as she thinks, since after all a miscarriage occurred. This is one of the unfortunate things in practice which the conscientious man must be willing to bear. His duty is to save the life of the child in iitero even if the mother is unwilling to undergo any sacrifices for its sake. Only exceptionally, as in syphilitic offspring or in tuberculosis of the mother, can this duty be laid aside.

But how long shall we persist in these efforts to check abortion? To answer this in a given ease requires experience and judgment. As Kuestner said recently in a discussion before the Breslau Gyne- cological Society (March 21, 11105), we cannot gauge such matters by the watch or the calendar. We must persist until our efforts to check uterine contractions have failed absolutely, or until developments show or point wnth strong probabilitj to the fact that the fetus is dead.

Kest is the absolute essential to success in the prevention of abortion. It is the only way in which we can prevent the further formation of thrombi in the placenta and allay the contractions of the uterine muscle. This rest consists of absolute confinement to bed for a period varying from four or five days to several weeks. The moment a bloody discharge appears the patient must be put to bed, and kept there until after the bleeding has entirely ceased for four days. Pains must also cease absolutely. It is best, wherever possible, to have patients use the bed-pan; but where bowel evacuations are inadequate in the recumbent posture, it may be permissible to have them get up to use the commode. As we frequently give morphine or other narcotics to these patients to check uterine contractions, attention to the bowels is one of the essentials to success. Hardly anything is more likely to lead to an abortion than the straining and pressure incident to a constipated bowel movement. Hence it is well to give moderate doses of cascara or pheuolphthalein, sufficient to cause one good movement daily.

External applications of various sorts have been recommended, but without much benefit. Cold compresses or an ice-cap over the abdomen seem as a rule rather to provoke pains than to check them. Warm cloths, on the other hand, have in some instances served to diminish the painful spastic contractions and may be employed where there is as yet no bleeding. Edgar recommends cold compresses to the vulva in case of abortion starting with a free hemorrhage. That there are exceptions to every rule is seen by the fact that in a few patients the use of the vaginal tampon has tended rather to check the abortion than to increase uterine contractions. It is for this reason that we find writers who recommend the tampon. The bulk of clinical experience, however, is opposed to its use as a prophylactic measure.

Coming now to the drugs, we find in opium and its derivatives our most valuable help. It must be given in liberal doses and for a considerable time. Where indications are urgent, morphine gr. 14 should be given hypodermically. Codeine gr. 12 to 34 every one to three hours until from two to six doses have been taken is recommended by some. Eeynolds pushes the opium until the patient is narcotized; then he stops, and, if the pains return, he repeats the opium as before. Bromides may be given in liberal doses, with viburnum, asafoetida or hydrastis.

Edgar suggests this prescription:
Sodium Bromide 16.0
Simple Elixir 96.0
Tr. Hyoscyamus 16.0
Extr. Viburnum 16.0
Two teaspoonfuls in water every three hours.
Kleinwaechter gives
Extr. Viburnum 3.0-5.0
Tinct. Opii 1.0
Aquae. Lauroe 5.0
Aquae. Naphae 25.0
Teaspoonful four times daily.

The use of ergot, as suggested by some men, must be condemned as a dangerous experiment. It will more often do harm than good. "Where the cause of the miscarriage is a cervical tear, the ergot may serve to cause a retraction of the remaining cervical libers and so help to check the expulsion of the ovum.

Naturally we must look to the psychic condition of our patients. They must be kept in a quiet, darkened room, as free as possible from any emotional disturbances. They should not be allowed to see visitors and the diet must be bland and rather light, so that digestion will not be disturbed. If there are no pains and the bleeding is but slight, they may be read to or entertained in some quiet way so that the time in bed does not hang too heavily on their hands. Household worries must be kept out of the sick-room. In fact, mental rest is of almost equal importance with physical rest in the prevention of miscarriage.

Prevention of Criminal Abortion 111 the chapter on "Frequency," the fact was brought out that about fifty per cent of all abortions were criminal. The yearly figures ill some of the larger cities of this country and abroad are ap)alling. It may, indeed, be said that it is the one crime that is almost universal, is found among all classes, in all countries. Even the savages are not exempt from it. One has only to glance through Ploess' book on "Woman" to see what a variety of instruments have been devised for its production since the beginning of history. Our daily press advertises with impunit, under the thinnest sort of veil, medicines that will "regulate" the flow and physicians or mid-wives who will licl)) those "in troulilo." It is a crime that is pun-

Figure 29 Iiistruuients used for purposes of criminal abortion. Tliis set was openly for sale in Paris, (v. Wint-kel.) ishable by a severe penalty, but is iractically never punished. Is it surprising, then, that we find an estimate of 80,000 criminal abortions a year in New York, 6,000 to 10,000 a year in Chicago, and like numbers elsewhere? Doleris gathered statistics showing that abortions were markedly on the increase in Paris. This doubtless applies equally to the rest of the civilized world, and the reason is not difficult to find. The discovery of asepsis and antisepsis has not proved any unmixed blessing. Criminal abortion can at the present time be done wdth less danger of blood-poisoning than formerly. The result is inevitable. One of the main deterrent factors in the production of abortion is gone when the woman realizes that her own life is not necessarily imperiled.

It seems probable that this question will become one of the most serious sociological problems of the coming years, for eveiy community must in self-preseivation enact laws and exert its utmost influence to stem this tide that will otherwise sweep it to destruction.

In what way can this be done? Primarily, I believe, along two lines: (1) Education. (2) Legislation.

(1) The need of education in matters medical has been generally recognized in recent years. On hardly any subject is ignorance more widespread than just on questions of this sort. The nij'tli that life does not begin until fetal movements are felt is still so widespread that it will take many years before it is finally put aside. Almost daily the physician hears tlie story that the woman did not think it was wrong to stop pregnancy in the early months before the child was alive. A forceful treatise on the "Moral and Legal Status of the Fetus in I'teio" was written by AV. II. Sanders a few years ago, in which just this error was emphasized. Women of all classes should know more concerning the j rocesses of gestation. They should be shown how early the fetal heart begins to pump blood through its vessels. They should be taught that in the first weeks, if not sooner, the sex is already determined. In connection with a series of medical lectures for women, which I arranged to have given in one of the social settlements of this city, the question of criminal abortion was discussed. For this purpose I instructed, the nurse who gave the lecture to show an enlarged picture of an embryo of six weeks. The fact that at this time the eyes, ears, nose, mouth and extremities were already crudely formed was the source of much amazement to these women. It is not enough merely to tell them that in producing an abortion in the early months they are taking a human life; they must be shown that at this period the eliild is already well along in its development. I think pictures like tliat of the six weeks' embryo will keep many women from having an nlior tion done.

In like manner we find the danger of blood-poisoning but little understood. The mortalitv of criminal abortion, even under modern ; intimiitii inct. li((ls, is still IVi iit Ililly hiyli. rcridratinn is not un-((timiinii; sepsis with fatal initc-ome is of frequcnl (icciirrcikn, and the (M-cciita,!;(' that have milder forms of infection with more or less resulting invalidism is fully 30 to 40 per cent, i believe that many women ean be prevented from committing an al)ortion)y exjilaining to them all the dangers involved.

(2) Legislation, or rather the enforcement of legislation, is still sadly inefficient in this country. The laws are on the statute books, but they either are not or cannot be enforced. Figures in New York show about one prosecution to a thousand criminal abortions. In St. Louis it is only a few times a year that a case comes up for trial and tlicu the chances aie ten to one against conviction even in the face of evidence tliat to any fair-minded person would be incontrovertible.

The fault lies primarily in the difficulty of obtaining the admission of evidence. In Missouri a recent statute provides that the dying declaration of the woman before witnesses can be used as evidence against the accused person. In fact, although the woman is a party to the crime, the only hope of exterminating these practices lies in the conviction and punishment of the individual who actually perpetrates the abortion.

In. the vast majority of instances the guilty party is a midwife or disreputable doctor. It is hoped additional legislation may produce favorable results. By making the requirements for medical practice more stringent, the number of physicians will be lessened and the average income raised, so that the temptation to do such work for money will be less often present. By the registration and proper examination of midwives even greater reform will result. Police control will be more readily effected and these pernicious practices will, to some extent at least, abate. Until a few years ago in Missouri, it was only a misdemeanor to do an abortion if the woman did not die. Now it has been made a felony. Life imprisonment is the extreme punishment for this offense.

It is to be hoped that before long laws will be enacted that will more ettectually protect the conimunity against the wholesale "Slaughter of the Innocents." Of late there has been a reversal of opinion in favor of a little more paternalism in our government. The government supervision of banks and trusts and other business affairs will, I believe, be followed by a stricter government super- vision ou matters of health. At present the matter of recording births is left to tlie community. It is essentially a matter of interest to the Federal government, for at each birth a future citizen of the Republic comes to life. In similar wise the State or Federal government should control the matter of abortions. I am firmly convinced that if every abortion, no matter what the cause, would have to be officially reported, it would prove a long step ahead in the way of correcting present evils. Moreover, independent of its effect upon this question, the government is entitled to know of the death of any living being, whether that being has advanced to full-term development or not. It is time that the antiquated ideas of modern law as to when life begins be moditied in accordance with our present knowledge. Life begins with conception.

The requirement of a burial certificate was an undeniable factor in lessening the frequency of murder; in similar wise the registration of every abortion would, I believe, materially reduce the number of criminal abortions.

A suggestion of considerable value made by Dorsett in his address as chairman of the Section on Obstetrics and Gynecology at Chicago, in 1908, was that more attention be i aid to the instruction of medical jurisprudence at medical schools, so that physicians would be more familiar with the statutes regarding criminal abortion, and would know what steps to take to bring gnilty parties to prosecution.

CHiu TER Xm

Treatment of Uncomplicated Abortion

Thero was a time, some years ago, when it was considered necessary or advisable to hasten to its termination every case of inevitable abortion. The moment the diagnosis was made, some form of operative treatment was advised. That such a position was extravagant is best shown by the fact that, after all, in a majority of abortion cases, the woman never consults a physician and yet does not meet with any bad consequences. Although frequently dependent upon pathologic conditions, the expulsion of the ovum, whether premature or not, is essentially a physiologic act, and if no complications ensue, it ought to be completed without difficulty.

It is hard for the doctor to decide just when it is incumbent upon him to interfere. Where abortion is clearly inevitable and contraction pains are coming on at regular intervals, it is well to apply heat to the abdomen in the form of a hot-water bag. Some writers recommend hot bichloride douches given two to three times a day. If the progress is steady, but not sufficiently rapid to suit the special exigencies of the case, we may tampon the vagina with iodoform gauze in alternating periods of twenty-four hours. Should such a tampon be employed in the cervix also, care must be taken not to rupture the membranes, as this would probably serve to render the expulsion more complicated.

Case 8. Elmira I, aged 24, had been married six years, and during that time had three children and one miscarriage. Her present trouble dated back to January 22, 1908, when she had had her last regular menstruation. Since that time she had complained of dizziness and occasional nausea, but no vomiting. In April she had pains in her back and lower abdomen. Vlien she came to see me, May 23, she stated that she thought she had had some fever for two weeks and that two days ago (at approximately tlie time of the menstrual wave, be it noted) a profuse bleeding began. The blood was clotted, and somewhat odorous. Eather severe cramp-like pains were present.

I examined and found a uterus of about four months' gestation, the cervix dilated to admit the finger, the vagina filled with clotted blood. She at once entered the Washington University Hospital and, as the bleeding was free, a vaginal tampon was put in place. During the night the pains became stronger and the entire ovum, with amniotic cavity and decidua intact, was expelled. (Fig. 14.) The subsequent course of the case was uneventful. There was no fever and the patient, against my advice, left the hospital on the seventh day, feeling perfectly well.

If the progress, in a given case, is satisfactory we may simply await developments, meanwhile keeping the jdatient in bed, ordering a moderately light diet, and paying attention to regularity of bladder and bowel evacuations. When the ovum has been expelled it is carefully examined and ojjerative indications based partly on the findings. Should a piece of placenta be found missing, we may, in the absence of fever or hemorrhage, treat expectantly for three to four days, in the hope that the remaining piece will come away spontaneously. If this does not occur, we must resort to digital removal.

If it is apparent that the entire ovum has been expelled from the uterus, we should as a rule refrain from interference. Should it still be lying in the vagina, we must remove it and the remaining hloodclots with the sterile finger. Ergot in the usual dosage is then given.

And here a word as to the use of ergot before abortion is completed, for the purpose of hastening its progress. Webster objects most strongly to the use of ergot at this time. His experience has been that it tends rather to retard than to hasten the complete expulsion of the ovum. There is apt to result a condition of cervical retraction which it is difficult for the uterine muscle to overcome. The giving of ergot at this time seems to predispose to the retention til the placeuta. Iii place of this drug, it is better to use heat or cold to)roiiiote uterine contractions. Some text-books recommend giving an antiseptic vaginal douche after every abortion, on the principle that in almost every case the expulsion has been incomplete and tlie oliauoe for infection considerable. Certainly, in a large majority of cases, this is true, for the antiseptic douche heads oft" the likelihood of later trouble. When, however, an abortion or miscarriage has been uncomplicated and complete, we must use our judgment as to the douche. In general practice, if no digital examination has been made, it is just as well to omit the douche altogether. Likewise, where a single examination has been made with every precaution as to asepsis, it is inadvisable to complicate matters by giving a vaginal irrigation. We must beware of doing too much.

After-Treatment

The after-treatineut of abortion will resemble to some extent that of full-term coufiuemeut. The patients need a prolonged bedrest varying from eight to foi; rteen days, in accordance with the month at which gestation was interrupted, and in accordance with the special complications that may have been encountered. Involution does not proceed with the same proi ortional rapidity as after a normal confinement, mainly owing to the fact that a few little shreds of placenta or bits of decidua are left, even when to all appearances the ovum has been completely expelled. These bits of tissue are absorbed or expelled without trouble to the patient, but their presence, to some extent, interferes with the retrogressive changes in the uterus. Hence, subinvolution frequently follows a miscarriage and leads eventually to chronic endometritis, retroversion and occasionally to some prolapse. On the other hand, there has been no stretching of the abdominal walls, nor has there been any marked increase in the size of the uterus. Consequently, after the patient is once out of bed, she can be allowed to resume her usual household duties considerably sooner than the customary six weeks puerperium of a full-term gestation.

There has been much talk, of late, in the journals abroad and in this coimtry, about the advantages of getting patients up and out of bed a few days after confinement. It would be as great a mistake to permit this after abortions as after confinements. Yet this does not mean that patients may not. under special circumstances, be allowed to sit up out of bed for ten to thirty minutes daily after the sixth or seventh day. These special circumstances imply that the case has run a normal course, and that the patient's surroundings can be controlled; . e., that she is in the hospital or has a private nurse at home. Under all other conditions we nnist advise strongly against getting her up early. If the patient is not in good general condition she should be given absolute rest in bed for two full weeks.

Once out. of lied, she should be told to stay within the limits of lut own rooui Ior; itu)ther week, and not until three weeks after the abortion has been completed, should she be allowed to go out of doors or to attend to any of her household duties. And here it should be renieiubered that when the placenta has been retained in considerable amount, it is best to count the beginning of the eight to fourteen days' rest from the day it is expelled or extracted manually.

Ward recommends that after the first day or two the patient be urged to lie as little as possible on her back, preferably in a sort of Sims' position, in order to keep the strain off the uterine ligaments and induce a return to the physiological position of anteversion. Attention to regularity of the bowels and to frequent evacuations of the bladder (five to six times a day) will also help materially to bring-about this result. Many a retroversion can doubtless be prevented by these precautions.

The giving of douches after miscarriage is an almost universal custom, at least after the second or third day. It is a less dangerous and a less painful procedure than after a full-term confinement, since there are usually no external or vaginal wounds after a miscarriage. The advantages of hot antiseptic douches are several: (1) they tend to limit any tendency to beginning infection; (2) they hasten expulsion of little retained particles of placental tissue; (3) they bring about the more rapid involution of the uterus. Under ordinary circumstances two lysol (12 per cent.) douches a day will be sufficient.

Ergot should be given in every case without regard to special indications. This would not be proper after confinements, but after abortions it is usually imperative. It must not be forgotten that one of the main stimulants to proper uterine involution namely, the nursing of the child is lacking in abortions. Hence we employ medicines with, less reluctance than otherwise.

The ordinary fluid extract of ergot contains, beside the essential principles, many inert and irritating substances. Where used hypo-dermioally it causes a marked induration at the point of injection and is often followed by an abscess. Ergotol and evgone are two more purified preparations. We have also Seca-cornin (La Roche) and Ernutin, more commonly used abroad. The essential point involved is to eliminate all unnecessary toxic materials from the original product (see Appendix D). Ergotol, ergone and ernutin are given in fifteen to thirty-drop doses. The powdered alkaloid ergotin can also be employed in the form of two to three-grain capsules given three to four times daily. Stypticin, and its allied product, Styptol, have been highly recommended as a uterine hemostatic. The dosage is one to two grains three to four times a day given in powders, capsules, or liypodermically. My favorite prescription where there is prolonged bloody discharge is

R Ergotin 4.0
Stypticin 3.0
Extr. Nucis "omieae 0.4
Capsulae No. 30. S. One capsule four times a day.

Hydrastis preparations and the supra-renal extracts also act upon the musculature of the uterus and bring about a more rapid return to the normal.

Operative Indications

Where opinions vaiy so widely as they do in the matter of active or conservative treatment of abortion, and wiiere so many weighty authorities are gathered on both sides, it is difticult to arrive at a just conchision. The; tiuth, as I see it, does not lie entirely witli either side. Certaiiilx tlic statement of Mcgregory, that in thirty years' practice he saw no case where rest and tamponade did not suffice, gives a wrong impression. It is not a question of what will suffice: it is a question of what will give the best results with tlie least risk to the patient. Equally extravagant is the statement of Casteran, that we can never be certain of protection against infection or hemorrhage in abortion, and hence sliould in all cases use operative methods of one sort or another before such complications have a chance to set in. He terms this, "Prophylaxc des accidents," the prophylaxis of complications. In this controversy, Ward has grouped the most prominent obstetricians into two camps, as follows: (1) Those favoring conservative treatment such as rest and tamponade: Lusk, Budin, V. Winckel, Tamier, Playfair, Zweifel, Stumpf, Etheridge, Parvin, Dohrn, Thomas, Eeynolds and Newell, Webster, and Williams.

(2) Those favoring immediate artiticial i-emoval of the ovum: Duehrssen, Braun, Muude, Doederlein, Pozzi, Garrigues, Fehling, Hirst and Edgar.

I quote from Edgar's Textbook the point of view of this second group of men:

"I advocate the active treatment of abortion, inevitable or incomplete, by reason of the analyses of the records of many hundreds of cases, treated by various methods, and especially from an exhaustive study of the pathology, bacteriology, duration, complications, sequelae and treatment of 242 cases; 166 of which were treated by instrumental curettage; 45 by combined instrumental and

Ore: BATIVK INDICATIONS. S9 digital curettage;:! by digital curettage only, aud 28 by a purely expectant treatment. Contrasting the expectant and active plans of treatment of abortion, I believe that the latter is less dangerous tlian the abortion aud its sequelae in cases of retention, and curettage makes sure that everything is removed; involution and time are uecessarj- for convalescence after abortion; the one is hastened, the other cut short, after curetting; this is of course a boon to the working classes. The expectant plan requires two weeks for itself alone; after instrumentation the patient may leave her bed on the fifth day, pain and physical discomfort, as well as mental perturbation, are less than in the expectant method; moreover, a large proportion of so-calied complete abortion cases are followed by hemorrhage, subinvolution, acute and chronic sepsis; hemorrhage is always greater with expectant treatment; not more than half an ounce is lost by instrumentation, before the fourth month. In the first two months and a half, emptying of the uterus can be accomplished with curettage alone, the canal admitting the finger with ditifficulty and pain if anesthesia is not used. ITterine atony is controlled by irrigation and uterine tamponade with gauze; ergot is rarely called for, the placental forceps only occasionally. If curettage for any reason cannot be accomplished at once the vagina may be tamponed with sterile gauze until the operation can be carried out. This course may also be pursued when curettage is refused, and the gauze packing may be left in for twenty-four hours. Again, if the accoucheur is a beginner, who dreads assuming the responsil)ility of forced dilatation and curettage, he is justified in adopting the conservative plan, and in temporizing with a gauze pack until dilatation occurs. Inevitable abortion may terminate, in a small number of cases, in expulsion of the ovum almost entire, in which case it is arrested in the cervical canal. Under these circumstances cui"ettage may not be necessary, as hemorrhage may cease after simple extraction witli the finger or forceps. In case the ovum is too large to pass through the os, the latter may be dilated."

It may be true, as "Ward says, that "because there are incompetent men, we should not teach incompetent methods;" nevertlie-less, we should not forget that the majority of aboi-tiou cases are treated by such so-called "incompetent" men. In fact, in taking the anamnesis of patients of the middle and lower classes I have been amazed at the frequency with which women pass unharmed through an abortion w. itliout any trealnienl wiiatsoevlT except rest in bed. The expert in surgical work is inclined to underestimate the dangers attendant upon every surgical procedure. What is simplicity itself for him is a matter of the greatest difficulty for most practitioners. What is perfectly safe in a clean operating room, is very dangoi-ous in- a squalid hut Yith insuiliciont light and an almost impossible asepsis. I have tried to set the operative indications in the following chapters, keeping constant!)- in luiud the fact that they are addressed primarily to the comparatively unskillful practitioner, and jet not forgetting that delay is at times more dangerous than operative interference. I should therefore summarize the operative indications thus: In the absence of immediate danger, await developments. Operate only when complications ensue.

Instrumentarium

Physicians usually attend miscarriage cases with but scanty provisions for taking care of their patients. It is not at all infrequent that a speculum, a dressing forceps, and either cotton or gauze, are all that have been brought along. In an emergency, of course, such an instrumentarium will suffice for performing a vaginal tamponade, but will not suffice for other operative measures. A number of the special instrument cases tliat have been put upon the market

Figure 30 Instrument case closed. The straps used to hold the case can. if necessary, serve as leg-holders.

are quite complicated and expensive. For this reason I have attempted to simplify some of the ideas already suggested in the constraction of a case that shall be both complete and inexpensive. The description of this instrument case will give an idea of the necessary instrumentarium for handling abortions. It is like a Japanese top, one thing inside the other. The instruments are placed in the tray used as an instrument sterilizer, and this tray is

The above instrument case can be obtained, either with or without the necessary instruments, from the Kny-Schecrer Co., 404 West 27th St., New York, or their agents.

JlikN I. NTION AXI) TREAIM i: 1 ol- A llokIKlx.

slipiunl iiisitleaii obloiis; (loucho-caii, tlms ronniiisi: a closed box, out of which tlie instruuieuts cauuot drop. This box is protected by a thin leather eoveriiifr, which buttons, and the whole is held together by a shawl-strap, Ihc stiaps (if wliicli aic luii. i; ciuiugh to liold back the patient's limbs, in case operative measures are necessary. The acconi ianyiug iuusti-ation will give an idea of the consti-uction of this instrument box.

jijm,

Figure 31 Instrument case open, showing sterilized tray, douche can, outer case with pocliet for suture material, rubber gloves etc. and the instruments necessary for the treatment of the various complications (see footnote on pre ious page).

The instruments necessary for the treatment of these eases are also to be seen in the accompanying photograph. They include, from left to right, the following articles:

Uterine packer.
Tenaculum forceps.
Uterine irrigator.
Goodell dilator.
Two dressing forceps (curved).
Ovum forceps. Large blunt curette. Large sharp curette. Small sharp curette. Operating Graves speculum. Kelly pad.

The uterine packer is a very valuable instrument where the cervical canal is still narrow. It is best to get one of medium size, so that a two-inch strip of gauze can be passed through it. The newest design of this packer has a small rod along its inner surface that prevents the gauze from being pulled out of the uterus as the instrument is withdrawn.

The tenaculum forceps that I prefer in my case is shown on following page. A similar instrument has been described by others. Its object is to enable one to work without an assistant when he is not obtainable. The forceps has twx) hooks so that it may be caught over the edge of the Graves speculum and in this way both hands are left free for other manipulations.

The uterine irrigator is of the ordinary Bozeman type. It must be constructed so as to give ample opportunity for a return flow of the injected fluid, since otherwise a portion of the fluid might pass through the Falloiiiau tube into the peritoneal cavity, and cause fatal results. A number of such accidents are on record.

Goodell's dilator or one of a similar type will occasionally prove necessary in the earlier months when the cervix is rigid and not well dilated. The amount of dilating pressure must always be carefully regulated, as the cervix of a pregnant woman tears readily under rajjid dilatation. Two dressing forceps are necessary to cleanse the vagina thoroughly and serve as sponge holders.

The ovum forceps should not be too long; ten to eleven inches is ample. They should have a pelvic curv(, and the grasping ends should be scooped out like a spoon curette, but with absolutely blunt edges and a blunt, rounded end. The ovum forceps is made without a catch at the handle, for it is intended merely to grasp things and not to clamp down upon them. One German modification goes even further and is so constructed that the grasping ends lack 12 cm. of coming together. By this means they cannot ordinarily pinch off tissue or otherwise cause damage.

The curettes sliowu in the illuf tration are of tlie usual blunt and sharp types. The blunt double spoon curette of Martin is much used abroad. One end has a diameter of 1.8 cms., and the other end 0.9 em. The ends of the instrument aio rounded off so as to diminish the chances of perforation.

I would sjieciall y recommend the use of a short-bladed self-retaining vaginal speculum. The type usually referred to as Graves

Figure 32 Instruments for treatment of abortions. A. = Graves short-bladed operating speculum; B. = Glasgow double-way intra-uterine irrigator; C. = Graduated cervical dilator; D. = Curved volsellum, with hooks for use as self-retaining instrument.

operating speculum will answer the purpose. The speculum must distend the vaginal outlet as much as the patient can tolerate, but at the same time should not in any way interfere with the movement of the cervix. If the speculum has long blades, traction on the cervix with tenaculum forceps will be hampered, and it will consequently be impossible to bring the cervix in line with the finger or curette. For all subsequent intra-uterine instriunentation this is essential. Another advantage of tliis speculum is that its flanges can be used to hold in place sterile towels and in this way cover np the labia and their hairy growth. This is a practical point of considerable value, particnlarly when circumstances make it difficult to obtain a thorough cleansing of the external genitals. The general arrangement of the patient with speculum in place is seen in the accompanying photogi-aph. (Fig. 3.3.)

Figure 33 Graves speculum in place. 11 is selt-ielaining and, being short-bladed, allows the cervix to be pulled down. The flanges to either side can be utilized to hold in place sterile towels covering the labia and pubic hairs.

Beside the instruments there should be included in this set the following articles:
A Kelly pad.
An apron, preferably of thin oiled cotton.
One pair of rubber gloves.
A chloroform mask.
Fil'ty gnuiis cliloroform.
Iitiiloride tablets.
Two ounces lysol.
Two hand-brushes.
Hypodomiic case, inclndini; ergot for hypodermic use.
One tube of iodoform gauze (two inches by three yards).
Small package of sterile absorbent cotton.

All these ai-ticles, except the Kell- pad and tlic apron, can be placed with tlie instruments in tlie box described above. The pad and ainon can be-)laced between the box and tlic canvas cover.

CHAPTEE XYll
Operative Technique

General Preparations. It is sui)risiiig witli svliat carelessness many inaetitioners undertake the management of a case of abortion. As Thomas truly says, "You will tind that many a man who conducts everything in a truly antise)tic manner when labor occurs at full term will neglect the same precautions in cases of abortion." We urge every practitioner who attends cases of this kind to have, if possible, an instrumentarium as described in the previous chapter, or at any rate to have the most necessary instruments, with gauze and cotton in a separate bag ready for use.

Abortion cases are usually, or at any rate frequently, emergency cases, and hence it is best to have everything ready for use at a moment's notice. A pair of rubber gloves is even more essential in this kind of work than in oi3s t e tr ics. Fortunately, in obstetrics, intra-uterine manipulations are rarely necessary, but in abortions they are very often indicated in order to ascertain whether the uterine contents have or have not been completely expelled. Consequently, infection is more apt to occur.

It has been stated that few patients bleed to death from hemorrhage during a miscarriage. Earely does the continued bleeding necessitate such hurry that aseptic precautions cannot be observed. The patient herself has usually made no preparations.

Room and bed are not arranged for the emergency. The first stej s, therefore, must be to protect the mattress and floor, and to put clean sheets upon the bed. The patient's abdomen, thighs and external genitals are thoroughly cleansed, the pubic hairs clipped or shaved, and fresh stockings and night gown put on. The bladder should be emptied and, if necessary, an enema should be given for the thorough evacuation of the bowels.

Upon the table next to the bed there should be the insti-ument tray, a basin with a one-half per cent, lysol solution, a basin with a 1 to 2,000 bichloride solution for the physician's hands, a one- iound roll of sterile absorbent cotton, a five-yard jar of plain io(h)form

PREVEXTIOX AM) THKA IM laI Ol ABORTION.

gauze, towels, etc. A two-quart fountain syringe or douche-can containing one-lialt per cent, lysol solution at about 112 F. sliould be in readiness.

AVhere o iorative measures are indicated, some operators prefer to place tlio iatieiit on a kitolien table, as tliis considerably facili-

Figure 3-1 Aiiiiuycinoiit of kitchun table preparatory to a ciirettement or digital removal of the placenta. (Crossen.) tates any necessary manipulations. There are, however, two sides to such extensive changes in household arrangements. More assistance is required to carry the patient to and from the table, to hold the legs during the operation, etc. We should prefer to limit the use of tlie table to those cases iu which special difficulties are expected and where narcosis is necessary.

Another point to consider is the advisability of taking the patient to u hosi)ital. Here we are of necessity bound to consider the iinancial condition of the patient. In primiparae where the absence of cer ical dilatation makes it likely that operative manipulations will be required, it is best to transport the patient to the hospital. Likewise, in cases in which aseptic preparations in the home caimot be carried out, or cases in which the light is insufficient or the after-care likely to be inadequate, we must urge our patients to go to a hospital.

Expression of the Ovum. The simplest of operative manipulations is the expulsion of tiie ovum by bi-manual expression, and yet

Figure 35 Budin's method of expressing the ovum. The uterus is pushed Into retroversion; then, with the two vaginal fingers as high posteriorly as possible and the abdominal fingers above, pressure is exerted from above downward.

it is one that must be correctly done in order to be efifective. Bndin, who first suggested this method, gave the following directions: The cervix should be well dilated. The ovum must be lying in the uterine cavity or in the cervical canal, freed from its attachment to the uterine wall. Two fingers of one hand are placed posterior to the cervix and the cervix pushed forward to the symphysis, thus causing a retroversion. The abdominal hand then grasps the uterus above and pushes it downward. The vaginal fingers at the same IKEYENTIOX AMI IKi: A IM i: X I OF AHOUI'ION.

tiim reacli jis lii li up; is K)ssil)l(along the i)()sttric)r wall of the uterus, and l)y ikiidiiii;-. make a movement of expression or milking toward the external os. if loosened from its attachment and not meeting obstruction in tlic ccrvical canal, the ovum will pop out of the uterus just as a pea does out of its pod. (Fig. 35.) Should the ovum be large it ma. v be necessary to bieak it into several pieces before expression will be possible.

A vaiiation of this procedure, accoiding to Iloening, consists in keejiing the uterus in an anteverted position and pressing witii the vaginal iingers against the anterior wall. (. Fig-) It is claimed that the fundus can be massaged more effectively in this position.

Figure 36 Hoening's method of expressing the ovum, similar to Budin's. except that the litems is kept in an anteverted position.

Tamponade. Depending on the special indications, we may tampon either the vagina alone, or both uterus and vagina. The tampon is used primarily to check hemorrhage, to stimulate uterine contractions, to promote dilatation of the cervix and to act as an antiseptic. The material used most frequently is five per cent, iodoform gauze. Since cases of iodoform intoxication have been reported, stronger preparations of iodoform gauze are not desirable and some even prefer to use in its stead plain gauze. Bichloride gauze must be used with great caution, since the absorptive power of the pregtiant uterus is considerable and salivation may result.

Technique of Vaginal Tamponade. In order effectually to check hemorrhage, the tampon must be placed in solid layers against the cervix. It is best to put in several strips, al)ont the size of the pnhu of the baud, and pack them firmly one against the other. Moist gauze packs tighter than dry. If the patient be a nullipara, a speculum will have to be introduced and the dressing forceps employed to pack in the gauze tightly about the cervix. In withdrawing the speculum, the forceps should hold the gauze in place, so as not to draw any of it into the lower part of the vagina. In fact, special care must be taken to avoid filling the lower third of the vagina, since there would otherwise Iesult retention or painful urination, a most annoying feeling of pressure, and finally increased liability to infection owing to the absence of the nonnal physiologic closure of the vagina.

Where the woman has had children and is not very sensitive, it is simpler and better to introduce two fingers into the vagina up to the cervix and under their guidance pack the gauze with the dressing forceps to the required amount in the vaginal fornices. We would especially warn against any attempt to pack in the gauze without the assistance of fingers or speculum, as this is excruciatingly painful and attended by great danger of carrying infectious germs from the vulvar hairs into the vagina.

The tampon should be left in place from twelve to twenty-four hours. It may occasionally be advisable at the end of that time to put in a fresh tampon. Whenever uterine contractions cease, it is an indication that the tampon should be removed. This can best be done with the finger, aided at times by the dressing forceps.

Uterine Tamponade. Excejit where we are doubtful of our asepsis, uterine tamponade is preferable to vaginal, since it is more certain in its effect and tends to loosen the entire ovum from its uterine attachment. The special indications for the uterine tampon are thus given by Chazan:

"(1) When the ovum is intact and the severe hemorrhage cannot be cliecked by a vaginal tampion, a cervical tampon will usually suffice.

"(2) In incomplete abortion and closed cervical canal.

"(3) In placental retention where the size of the uterus leads one to expect difficulty in digital extraction, or where some assistance may still be exjiected from uterine contractions: a condition that, according to Duehrssen, is more likely to ensue where jiregnancy is far advanced.

'(4) 111 lioinonlia. ne after partial difiilal rciiioxal of a retained IDlacenta, when hits ol iilacoiital tissue i-aii still he Ielt with the linger-ti, but i-auuot be removed owiug to the exhaustion of the l)hysician and the absence of nnreosis. Here the beginner may use the tampon in place of the curette. It protects against hemorrhage for the time being, and the remaining piece will usually be found clinging to the tampon when it is removed the next day."

Case No. 9. The successful use of the uterine tamponade is well illustrated by the following history: Mrs. J. B. L., a woman of thirty, whose previous pregnancies consisted of one full-term child eight years ago and (Hic miscarriage five years ago, had had her last menstruation in. luly, 1907. In September she was suddenly seized with a sjiontaneous uterine hemorrhage and at once sent for me. I found the cervix dilated to admit one finger, and after two days' persistent bleeding in spite of rest and opiates, I packed the uterus and vagina with iodoform gauze. On removing the pack twenty-four hours later, fetus and placenta were found lying in the vagina with the gauze. The cervix was wide open and the finger could easily be inserted. Exploration revealed the uterus entirely empty. Ergot and rest were prescribed and the recovery was uncomplicated.

Technique of Uterine Tamponade. Special precautions must be observed in placing a tampon in the uterus to avoid any contamination of the gauze by the external genitals. For this reason it is best to use one of the so-called uterine packers already described, by means of which the gauze never comes in contact with the vulva, but passes from the sterile glass container through the tube of the packer directly into the uterine cavity. (Fig. 37.) After the cervix has been exposed with a speculum, its anterior lip is caught with the volsella. The packer, into which a strip of gauze reaching just to the upper end of the tube has been placed, is then introduced into the uterine cavity. Care must be taken not to introduce it too far. Then the gauze, which should be one-half to two inches in width, depending upon the size of the uterine cavity, is caught with the pronged rod in the tube and packed bit by bit into the cavity until the latter has been filled. Care will have to be taken in the use of the packer to be sure that the rod goes all the way in each time, as otherwise the ganze may heeonie eiogged iu the tube. It would be well for those unfamiliar with its use to practice with the packer on some cloth pocket so that in time of emergency they will be prepared to use it properly.

If no packer is at hand, or if the uterine cavity is large and the cervix fairly well dilated, wo can pack in the gauze with the ordinary

Figure 37 Photograph illustiatlng the use of the gauze packer. If there is no assistant the tube containing the gauze can lie on the doctor's lap. while the left hand steadies the cervix with the vulsella forcept".

uterine packer used in curettements, or even an ordinary dressing forceps.

After as nuicli gauze as possible lias been put into the uterus, the usual vaginal tampon is also employed. The uterine tampon should be left in place twelve to twenty-four liours. It not rarely happens that the uterine gauze, togetlier with tlic ovum or retained placenta, will be found lying in tlic vagina the next morning, or it

OrkRATIVE TECHXIQIK.

may happen that iu removini the uterine packing the piece of retained placenta will be found clinging to its meshes and thus is extracted-witliout further difficulty.

Technique of Cervical Dilatation. "While the simplest and best method of cervical dihitatinii is the gauze tampon, we may at times

Figure 39 The use of the eenical dilator. The index finger must always be placed at such a point that the dilator cannot slip beyond the cervical canal. In this way perfoi-ation can be avoided.

liiul it advisiible lo. suppkiiicnl n with other inethod. s. Ucca-sioiuiuy the cervical canal is entirely chised, so that the gauze packer camiot be introihiced. I'his is esi)ecially the case in lher.-i i(Mitie-induced abortions in nulliparous women. Here it is best to use either laniinaria tents or graduated metal dilators. (Fig.-i.) The lamiuaria tent nnist be used with extia precaution, as several cases are on record in which the tent sli ii)ed into the uterine cavity and was e. xtrat'te(l oidy with gieat diniculty. The danger of infection from the teut is also considerable. It should be removed after 12 to 24 hours. Its only advantage is that it causes less pain and hence does not necessitate a narcosis. With metal dilatation an anesthetic will usually have to l)e given. The graduated dilators must be introduced gently and not too far for fear of perforation.

When the cervical canal has been stretched to a diameter of one and a half centimeters by this method, a gauze strip can be inserted into the cervix and firmly packed there, thus stinnilating further dilatation. It usually suffices in the first three months if the canal is large enough to admit one finger: that is to say, if it is two oi- two and a half cms. in diameter. If the o)erative ju-ocedure is to be effected with the curette instead of the finger, a diameter of 1.5 cms. will be sufficient and no gauze tampon need be employed. It is best to employ this method only in alh:)rtions u to the third month.

Technique of Dilatation with the Bag. Where the pregnancy has lasted three to five months and the ceivical dilatation is insufficient, the Champetier-de-Eibes or Voorhees bag can be used with good effect. The technique of this method (Fig. 40) is a little more cumbersome than that of uterine tamponade, but its effect is more certain and quick. Where we are anxious to end the abortion as rapidly as possible, and where other methods have failed to give the necessary dilatation, bag dilatation should be used. The inelastic bag, which has generally replaced the old elastic form of Barnes or Brann bags, can be sterilized by boiling or steaming for five minutes, or it may be brushed with a 1 to 2,000 bichloride of mercury solution, and immersed in the solution for one hour. The size of the bag to be employed will depend upon the stage of the pregnancy. In the third month, one whose greatest diameter is three cms. should be used. In the fifth month the diameter should be about six cms. The amount of water necessary to dilate the bag to its fullest capacity should be measured before introduction.

OPERATIVE TECHXIQI"

After the bag, a speculum, teuaeulum forceps, gloves, aud glass syringe of 100 c. e. capacity have been sterilized and a piut of warm sterile boric acid solution has been placed in a sterilized basin, the patient may be placed with her hi is at the edge of the l)ed and pre-

Figure 40 Introduction of m small Voorhees bag dilator into the cer ix.

pared in the same way as foi- the introduction of the tampon. The speculum is introduced and the posterior lip of the cervix caught with the teuaeulum. Some cervical dilatation is necessary to admit the bag, and, if not present, it must be brought about either digitally or bv means of metal dilators.

il. KXTIOX AND IKi; AI. MI. N r ol AlioHl'loN.

I'lic l)!!!" IS tlieii IouUhi, c.-mnlit with tlie i()itoi)s at its upper end and mntiy introduced until it lies just within the uterine cavity. (Fig. 41.) Tlie bag is then slowly tilled with the solution by means of the glass syringe. If the capacity of the syringe is insufficient, two syringefuls may have to be used. Only after this has been done should the forceps used in tlio introdnction be removed, one blade at a time, in this way the bag remains in position. A digital exami-

Figure 41 Small Champetier de Ribes bag introduced in a case of four months' abortion to hasten the dilatation of the cervix and promote expulsion of the ovum.

nation will generally reveal whether the bag lies within the cavitj. The membranes should be ruptured before introducing the bag, as there is otherwise danger of over-distending the uterus. Over-dis-tention causes severe pains, but insufficient contractions. If the use of the speculum seems to make the introduction more dithcult, it can be dispensed with and, after the tenaculum is caught, the bag slipped over the two vaginal fingers into the cervical canal. Where the vagina is narrow or where there is considerable bleeding, this procedure is preferable.

After introducing tlie bag it is best to give a hot antiseptic douche (one-half per cent, lysol), put on a T-binder and put the patient back into position.

"Where it is advisable to hasten dilatation, this can be accomplished by using gentle traction upon the end of the bag or attaching thereto a weight of two to three pounds swung over the end of the bed.

Technique of Digital Removal. U the puntaneous efforts of the uterus, or the various forms of tamponade, have not emptied the uterus, the digital removal of the ovum, or the portions of it still remaining;;; iitcro. becomes necessary. For this purpose thorough dilatation of the cervix is essential. "We must, in abortions up to the third month, have dilatation sufficient to admit one finger. In abortions from the fourth to the sixth mouth dilatation to admit two fingers will be necessary.

The (piestion as to whether narcosis is required for digital removal will depend largely upon the sensitiveness of the patient. Some patients suffer but slightly under the necessary manipulations. The doctor will, however, work more rapidly and with greater calmness if the patient is anesthetized. Occasionally the anemia of the patient or her unwillingness to take a general anesthetic, will make one decide in favor of a hypodermic of 14 gr. morphine with 1120 gr. atropine.

Special care should be taken as to asepsis of the external genitals and the hands of the accoucheur. As a rule the latter had better wear gloves, but I believe that for the first four or five times that; i physician is called to a case of this kind he had better scrub his hands more thoroughly and, unless he has been exposed to an infectious case, dispense with gloves. It is not easy to loosen the placenta from its attachment with one finger through a cervix that barely admits of. its entrance, and gloves make the work more difficult.

THE PREVENTION AND TREATMENT OF ABORTION 57

"When all necessary preparations have been made, the anterior lip of the cervix is caught with a medium-sized volsellum. I prefer this to the longer one more commonly used since it is less in the way during subsequent manipulations. Fixing the cervix with the volsellum in one hand, the middle finger of the other is introduced into the uterus, and the cervix

Figure 42 Digital extraction of the placenta (step one). "Fixing the cervix with the volsellum in one hand, the middle flnger of the other is introduced into the uterus and the corvix pulled over the finger as if it were a glo' e."

OPERATIVE Tr-: rhXigr k.

J) 111 led ()V(M the Iiuger as if it were a glove. (Fig. 42.) Then the handle of tlie vol so limn is canglit by the thumb of the v a g i ii a l h a n d. av h i i e the other h a n d o v er the abdomen (the latter covered with a sterile towel) seeks to press the f a n d i; s of the uterus down u ion the finger in the uterus. (Fig.-W.) If the ovum

Figure 43 Photogiaph illustrative of tlio Jiasianiniatic drawing of step one (Figure 42) in digital removal of the placenta.

is still present, it will be felt as a round object fastened at one or more points. If these be loosened and the ovum broken into several pieces, they can usuallj" be expressed by Budin's method, or, if necessary, hooked out one by one by means of the uterine finger. More commonly only a)ortion of the placenta will be Ietaiued. Here the finger feels one side smooth and the other covered by larger or smaller polyp-like excrescences. These can be freed from their attachment to the uterine wall and withdrawn either bv hook- g-.-

Figure 4(Digital removal of the placenia (step two). "Then the handle of the volsel-lum is caught by the thumb of the vaginal hand, while the other hand over the abdomen seeks to press the fundus of the uterus down upon the finger in the uterus." By rolling the finger from side to side the placental pieces are loosened and can then be hooked out one by one.

iiig the finger over them or with tlie assistance of a phacental forceps. Occasionally the uterine cavity will have an hour-glass shape owing to the fact that the portion of the uterus containing the placenta becomes partly pocketed off by the uterine contractions. (Fig. 46.) Such a contraction ring results with greatest frequency if ergot has been given, and mav interfere to a considerable extent with the

Figure 45 Photograph illustrative of the diagrammatic drawing of step two (Figure 44) in digital removal of the placenta.

digital extraction of placental pieces. After all the pieces have been loosened and the uterus emptied, the jjlacental site will still feel a little rough, but tliere will no longer be any great irregularities over its surface. It is only then that the operator should feel content, for the assurance that the uterus is really entirely empty of its contents means a great deal to the peace of mind of both . rbEVENI'loX AND TlikATM l-. XI OK A lioliliOX.

i:)atient; m(l jtliysiciaii. Tlu iii. sjxctiiui nl tlic iiiices expelled is usually very insullicient evidence on this Hiiiit. The dinitnl exploration ol" the uteiine cavity, on the other liaiid., i-ives; in nhiiost certain answer to the qnestioii.

Tt shonkl not be inuiiiiiied, however, lliat dij; ilal removal, or "curage," as the French call it, is an easy procedure. It is much safer tliaii instrumental metliods, but it

58 THE PREVENTION AND TREATMENT OF ABORTION

is alsd moic diffuiilt. T should advise all who have occasion to do nuich of this work to train tlieir fiiio-ers at every opportnnilv in obtainino- the r((iiisite

Figure 46 Hour-glass contraction of the uteius with retained placenta, a condition often resulting from the use of ergot. (. R. = ("ontiaction Ring; I. O. = Internal Os; E. O. = External Os.

skill in i)alpation. At times, however, even skilled jjcrsons will meet with such difficulties as to compel them to use other methods. In verj" fat women, for instance, it may be impossible, even in narcosis, to grasp the fundus of the uterus with sufficient firmness. At times the vagina may be too small to permit the necessary manipulations or the cavity of the uterus may be so large that the finger cannot reach its top. Here, more than in any other work, the man with the long slender finger will have a great advantage over the man with the short thick one.

Above all, in digital removal the operator should not allow himself to lie flurried by bleeding. Empty the uterus and it will stop. Only where the atient is anemic from previous hemorrhages will it be necessary to pack the uterus with gauze and wait for the remaining)ieees to come away spontaneously. Ordinarily, however, the bleeding in digital removal is less than in instrumental removal, since the finger acts in a way as a tampon to check the bleeding.

Where the uterine cavity is still large, as in abortions from the fourth to the sixth month, it will be necessary to insert two fingers into the uterus instead of one, in order to reach the fundus. (Fig. 47.) Since the cervix is more dilatable in the more advanced pregnancies, this additional dilatation is usually obtainable without special difficult. Occasionally, however, a tear occurs, as in the following-case:

Case No. to. Mrs. B. B., aged 33. had had five children and no miscarriages. The last child was born fourteen months ago. She consulted me May 1, 1908, stating that four months ago her menses had returned attended with some pain and clotted blood. In February and March there was no flow. In the first half of April there was on two occasions bleeding for a day; since April 1!), a continuous bloody discharge. Some pains in the back and lower abdomen since the last attack of bleeding. I found the vagina to contain some clotted blood, the cervix barely admitting a finger-tip, and the uterus, globular and soft, corresponding in size to a four months' gestation. Temperature, i)l) degrees. The patient was put to lied and given Codeine gr. 11 3x daily. The bleeding became less for a few days, but on May 8, one week later, the bleeding again liecame worse and the temperature rose to!)!.8 degrees. Fearing a beginning infection, I had the patient sent to the hospital. Her temperature on entering, Iay!), was 100 degrees, rising to 101.4 at 2 p. m. on the same day. At 4 o'clock I decided that the uterus would have to be emptied. Under ether narcosis I dilated the cervix manually, so that two fingers could be introduced. Then the membranes were ruptured and the legs of the fetus pulled through. As the head was a trifle too large to be extracted through the cervix, it was cmislied and the fetus removed)iecemeal witli the forceps. There was a profuse hemorrhage and the pu ceuta had to be extracted as rapidly as jossible. In so doing there was a slight extension of the cervical tear previously existing. The blood gushed out in large quantities as soon as the fingers were withdrawn from the uterus, in spite of the fact that the entire placenta had been removed and the walls of the uterine cavity felt smooth. A strip of plain gauze several yards long was packed into the uterus in order to check the atony of the uterus. In conclusion, the cervical tear was approximated by two sutures. The temperature of the patient ran up to 101.6 degrees that evening, falling to normal the next day. The subsequent course was uneventful; the patient left the hospital eight days later.

It is most exasperating when, after loosening the pieces of placenta, the efforts of the finger to hook tliem out of the uterus are unsuccessful. They, slijj away and turn around in the uterine cavity like a pool-ball in its pocket. Here it is necessary to seek the aid of the placental forceps.

Technique of Removal by Placental Forceps. The different kinds of placental forceps have been described in the previous chapter. The essential feature is that they should be sufficiently blunt, should have some pelvic curve, should have a rounded top, should not be too long and should not have a lock. Primarily the) la cental forceps is not intended for the loosening of the placenta, but for the removal from the uterine cavity of the pieces alreadj loosened. Usually it will be l)est. if placental forceps are to be used, to introduce a short bivalve speculum, or, in case there is an assistant, a posterior vaginal retractor, so as jiroiierly to expose the cervix. The volsella forceps is applied to the anterior lip and the uterus drawn more into the axis of the vagina. Then the placental forceps is introduced slowly through the cervix into the uterine cavity, and tlie size of the cavity measured. Approximately this has already been done bj the previous bimanual examination. This distance should be measured by the finger on the instrument and care taken never to introduce it beyond this point. While the abdominal hand from above tries to expel the loosened contents from the uterus just as in a Crede placental expression, thus forcing them into the region of the internal OS the placental forc(is is intrfklucod to this ioiiit. opetioil.

closed, and withdrawn. (Fig. 48.) This is repeated several times, and usually, on each occasion, some of the material will be exli-aeted. A renewed digital examination of the uterine cavity will reveal whether it is empty, and whether or not the ju-ocess will have to be repeated. Sometimes for the reasons already mentioned the control by digital examination cannot be effected. Here we should be satisfied if, after repeatedly introducing and withdrawing the instrument in the manner described, nothing more comes away. To a certain

Figure 49 Showing the position of the curette in the uterus. In a case of abortion the uterus would be about twice as large as in this figure. The curette must be held gently as a pen and only slight pressure exerted in scraping. (Crossen. t extent, we are of course "iishiug in tlie dark," but if done under the above precautions this will not be attended by danger of perforation or infection.

Some writers have recommended using the placental forceps to loosen the placenta from the walls of the uterus. After introduction, the blades of the forceps are opened wideh swept around the uterine cavity and then closed, grasping the material that has thus been loosened. This is repeated as often as material comes away. In certain cases of adlierent placenta, the forceyis has been advo- IUKVKNTION AND TKl ATMENT OF AUOHTION.

cated lor ijic imrpose dl iincliiii, i; dlv tlic plarciital tissiiu after its location has Ixcn cxacllx (Ictcnniiicd l)v digital exploration. Such mauipuiations must, however, be avoided by those who are not expert in the nianagement of tliese cases, and even in skilled hands they are occasionally attended by perforation.

Technique of Curettage. The technique of a curettage after abortion dilvcrs in many ways from that of a curettage for endometritis. It is specially indicated in early abortions with a rather small uterine cavity and comparatively firm uteriiu walls, in

Figure 50 Instruments needed for ordinary curettage. Speculum (a); dressing forceps (b. d); volsella (c); sound (e); small dilator (f); uterine dilator (g); large and small curettes (h. i); scissors (j). (Crossen.) cases of placenta retained some time after the expulsion of the fetus, and occasionally in adherent placenta as an aid to the finger in loosening the placental attachment.

Good light and a lateral position in bed are requisite. The speculum is introduced and the anterior lip of the cervix caught with the volsellum. The depth of the uterine cavity is determined with a sound, or with curved dressing forceps, great care being taken not to use any force, and to stop at once if the instrument penetrates further than the estimate of the depth of the cavity obtained by bimanual palpation. A sharp curette should be used only if a-neek or ten days have elapsed since the expulsion of the ovum, when, in other words, we may assume that the uterine walls are fairly firm in consistency. At other times the ordinary dull curette or the blunt-edged spoon curette of Orthmann should be used. The curette is introduced, and the placental site at once becomes evident from the fact, that it is uneven and soft as the curette glides over it. All manipulations must be made gently and without undue haste. The curettage should be localized to the placental site and should concern itself merely with the removal of placental pieces. It is not at all necessary for the little particles of decidual tissues to be scraped away. They will come away or be absorbed in the normal process of involution. The blunt spoon curette has been highly recommended as a safe and practical instrument for this work. After such a curettage it is usually well to give an intrauterine douche. This is particularly true of the septic cases, in which it is best to precede the curettage with a douche as well as to give one subsequent thereto. An iodoform gauze drain should be placed in the uterus.

Technique of Ecouvillonnage. Ecouvillon nage, or brusliiug the uterine ea ity, is a method used almost exclusively in France, but with such apparent success that its greater adoption in this country should be furthered. A brush (Fig. 51) like that used for cleaning test-tubes 'bristie btu s'irempioyed is employed for the purpose of loosening smaller " ecouvnionnage. fragments of placental tissue, p a r t i c u l a r l y in septic cases. The directions for its use are as follows: In deep narcosis remove larger pieces of placenta, digitally. Then give a weak bichloride douche. Brush out with the special brush; explore to see if the uterus is empty and the walls smooth. Eepeat this several times if necessarj Then brush out with a solution of Cresol and glycerine in the proportion of 1 to 5. Drain with iodoform gauze.

Technique of Intra-Uterine Douche. In certain septic oases it is advisable to nlve an intia ntiiine douche. I or this purpose one must be sure to use a two-way sterilizable douche-nozzle. The doiiclie-baii and tube must be boiled as well as the nozzle. The metal douche-nozzle ordinarily used has a guide to mark the depth to which it is to be introduced. This guide is regulated in accordance with the approximate size of the uterus as determined binian-ually. i'he douche-can or bag should be placed not higher than one foot above the bed, so as not to have too high a pressure. The solution sliould vary in amount from two (piarts to a gallon, should have a temperature of 105 to 112 F., i)referably tlu latter, and be made antiseptic by some less toxic material such as lysol (12) or alumi-nimi acetate (14) rather than carbolic acid or bichloride. The patient may remain pr-one in bed on a douche-pan. After preparing the external genitals, the cervix is caught with a tenaculum forceps under the guidance of the vaginal finger, some of the douche being used to cleanse the vagina, and then, using the tenaculum to steady the uterus, the doiiche-nozzle is gently passed along the finger in the cervical canal until its point lies just beyond the internal os. The water is then allowed to flow slowly, paying special attention to the return flow, and moving the end of the nozzle from side to side to insure against any blocking in the flow of tlie douche. Such a douche may be given daily if necessary. One of the essentials is that the uterus be disturbed as little as possible, since, otherwise, the infection may spread from the endometrium to deeper structures, and the douche thus do more harm than good. Some writers Iecom-mend slight pressure with the abdominal hand so as to correct the anteverted position of the uterus, and thus make a thorough irrigation easier. If the douche-nozzle is in accordance with the pelvic and uterine curve it can be more readilv introduced.

CHAPTER XVIII

Complications and Their Treatment

Hemorrhage

The amount of hemorrhage iu a ease of abortion is rarely so severe as to cause the immediate death of the patient. Tlie danger is rather from the persistent bleeding that causes severe anemia and predisposes to septic infection. The ainount of bleeding may, however, be so profuse as to soak clothing and bed. If the vaginal outlet is small, the blood may collect in the vagina and, being expelled later as a fountain of blood, give the impression of a very severe hemorrhage. It is difficult to judge in a given case just how much blood has been lost. AVe should be guided rather by the general condition of the patient. If the pulse becomes more rapid, rising to over 120 beats a minute, if there is cold sweat, dizziness, iiallor and, above all, restlessness, we can be certain that the hemorrhage has been a severe one and that everything must be done to offset the loss of blood as rapidly as possible.

The cause of the hemorrhage must first be determined. It will almost always be found in the retention of a portion of placental tissue. Less frequently do we have purely atonic bleeding and then usually after an anesthetic has been given. Where the ovum has not yet been expelled the hemorrhage is due to early dislodgment of the placenta from its site. Finally, we must not forget that a common source of hemorrhage in abortion cases is a deep cervical tear resulting from too rapid dilatation of the cervix in the efforts at extracting the ovum or its parts. The cervix of a pregnant uterus will often tear with great ease.

The treatment will depend on the special conditions to be met. In general, if we receive a telephone message to come at once to a case of hemorrhage from abortion, we should give some immediate instructions to the family: The hips of the jiatient should be ele- vated; the foot of tlie bcnl should be raised; pillows taken from the head; an ice-bag placed over the lower abdomen; the thighs kept tightly pressed together, so that the blood in the vagina may act to some extent as a tampon checking the uterine bleeding. If the bleeding is still severe, a relative or friend may apply pressure with the fist over the navel, compressing the abdominal aorta to some extent. To give ergot in these cases is rarely permissible, since there is usually something left in the uterus and the resulting contraction of the cervix makes it more difficult to remove the retained pieces.

Tlio physician, if he does not own the set described in Chapter X l, should have ready for such an emergency the following instruments: Speculum, tenaculum forceps, dressing forceps, uterine gauze packer, scissors, two artery forceps, a hypodermoclysis needle, cervix needle and thread, douche-nozzle of glass or metal, and rubber gloves.

There should also be on hand live yards of plain sterile or iodoform gauze, a one-half pound roll of sterile absorbent cotton, half a dozen towels, a clean sheet, boiled douche-bag or douche-can and at least two hand basins.

Of medicines he should take along some preparation of ergot for hypodermic use after the uterus is empty, lysol, chloroform or ether, bichloride tablets, tablets for salt solution, and the usual hypodermic tablets and syringe.

After the necessary external preparations an examination should reveal the progress of the case and the cause of the hemorrhage. If the patient is not in a hospital or where she can receive attention immediately, it is best, even if the bleeding has ceased on the arrival of the physician, to guard against its i-ecurrence by a tirm vaginal or utero-vaginal tamponade. A hot vaginal douche at 50 centigrade (122 F.) will check bleeding absolutely, but cannot often be tolerated. About 115 F. is the highest most women can stand. Of course, if possible, the surest and quickest way to check the bleeding is to empty the uterus, but for this purpose there must be sufficient dilatation and the condition of the patient must be such that she can stand the rather severe strain of digital removal. If she is very anemic or in shock, it is usually best to tampon and wait till the following day for her condition to improve. A beginning infection, however, should predispose one against further delay.

If the bleeding is atonic, brisk massage of the uterus should be exercised bi-maniially and the fingers used as a temporary plug until strips of gauze can be cut and tied one to another so that the entire uterine cavity is firmly packed. When the uterine cavity is rather rapidly emptied before the onset of vigorous uterine contractions, as in tlierajdeutie abortion, we are likely to get such atonic bleeding. A hypodermic of Ergone or Ernutin (see Appendix D), will also help to check bleeding. An ice-cap may be kept on the abdomen and pressure against the aoi'ta exercised.

Case No. 11. Mrs. C. D., aged 37, had had four children, the last one five years ago, and one miscarriage of five weeks' gestation occurring three years ago. Just previous to the miscarriage she had been operated on for lacerated cervix. Menstruation was regular, five to six days in duration and not painful. In June, 1906, there was only a sliow of blood. After that a blood-tinged discharge up to August 30th, when bleeding was more profuse. Clots of blood were passed, and she was j ut to bed by her physician. On September 17th there were passed several pieces partiall. v decomposed and odorous. Hardly any flow afterwards, but a continued blood-tinged discharge. From the middle of September on there were occasional dull aching pains in the lower abdomen. On October 20th there passed a piece of congealed blood, finger-like, associated with more profuse bleeding for six days. On November 16th there again appeared a free, non-odorous flow like a menstruation. The bleeding lasted from November 16th to 21st, and then stopped. That evening while bathing she had a few cramps. Suddenly at 10 o'clock, while at the theater, she was seized with a profuse hemorrhage. She was taken home and her physician simimoned. He found her almost pulseless and packed the uterine cavity with gauze. The following morning I was called and found the patient rather pale, but with a pulse of fair volume. Examination showed that just within the cervical canal lay a piece of placenta. The uterus was as large as an orange. Having placed the patient sidewise in bed, I introduced my finger under partial anesthesia and hooked out a piece of placenta larger than the palm of my hand, rather firm in consistency and without any evidence of decomposition. No trace of the fetus was to be found and even the site of the umbilical attachment could only be guessed at. At the time this removal was effected there was no rise of temperatui-e. The removal was altoinlod by very little luiiionliage and iiu pain. A curettemeiit with the dull curette followed tiiis operation. There were no complications whatever in the ai'ter-treatment.

It is of special interest to note that in this case the placenta was retained two and one half months after the expulsion of the fetus witliout causing any infection. (See Appendix B.) If the bleeding is due to a cervical tear, we must pack not merely the uterus, but also the u)))er hall of the vagina around the cervix with a firm tampon. At times sutures will have to be placed to check the bleeding. Krgot will also be of some aid in these cases when given hy)oderniically.

To combat the associated anemia it is best to give a hypodermo-clysis of 1,000 c. c. of normal saline solution under the breasts as soon as ijossible. The Murphy drop method of instilling salt solution into the rectum can be used additionally, and from 1,000 to 3,000 c. c. of water given, depending upon circumstances. The foot of the bed should be elevated, the pillow removed and a firm binder, with a pad exerting some jiressure on the abdominal aorta, but leaving the respiratory movements unhindered, should be applied.

Retained Placenta

Retained placenta is the most frequent of the complications of abortion. Out of Sittner's 302 cases in whicli operative measures were necessary, the entire ovum was retained 31 times, the placenta 201 times, and in 70 instances only portions of jilacental tissue. The dangers of retained placenta are threefold: hemorrhage, decomposition and infection. Fortunately these dangers are not so great during the first half of pregnancy as they are after delivery at full term. Hemorrhage, for instance, is practically never fatal at tliis time. Decomposition of the i lacenta does not usually set in unless retention has been prolonged for several days. Infection does not spread so rajtidly at this time as it does in more advanced pregnancies.

Retained placenta is not infrequently due to the mistake of the accoucheur in trying to remove the ovum when the cervix is not well dilated. The fetus and part of the placenta are within reach; they tear away from the rest when pulled upon and the balance remains in the uterus. When the membranes are unruptured it is less likely to occur. The taking of ergot will also increase the chances of placental retention, since it causes the cervix to contract before the uterine contents have been completely expelled. Where the jjlacenta is adherent on account of infarction, deciduitis, syphilis, etc., retention is very a it to occur. According to Rimette, in abortions of the third or fourth month the placenta is retained in one out of every five cases.

The pathologic changes undergone by the i)lacenta when it is thus retained require a few words of consideration. Naturally there is considerable disturbance of its blood su iply, so that ordinarily we find necrosis setting in within a rather short time. The small area of attachment is usuall y insufficient to nourish the entire placental area and degeneration sets in rapidly. This, by causing thrombosis of the decidual vessels, affects the adherent portion, so that within five or six days the placenta has changed to a dark-red, i, i; i: i: xti()X and tkeatmknt of ahokiion.

luusliy, frial))! mass, liaviiii a)ruik)uricc(lly Joul (uloi. Since the cervix remains jiartially open as lonj" as tlii phu-enta is retained, the cliance for npward spread of bacteria rroni the vagina is considerable. Sapropliytes quickly 7niihipl in this necrotic material, so that microsco)ically we usually lind evidence of marked leucocytic infiltration and many bacteria. Slmuld there be septic bacteria in the vagina these may tliroui li tlie favorable medium furnished by placental retention cause dangerous, even Jatal, infections. On the other linnd, a Iaceiita may at limes be retained in the uterus for a -:3: i–C. f:

Figure 52 Chorion villi, partially necrotic, from a case in which the placenta was retained nine months (Case 12). The villi, imbedded in a mass of coagulated fibrin, have lost almost their entire syncytial cover and show necrobiosis of the connective tissue. N. V, = Necrotic Villus; C. F. = Coagulated Fibrin; Syn. = Syncytium.

long period without the slightest decomposition. The only changes undergone are shrinking due to desiccation, and a slow necrobiosis with infarction of the tissues. This is very well seen in the specimen (Fig. 52) taken from Case 12, whose history is as follows:

Case No. 12. Mrs. D., 35 j-ears old, gave a historj of having had "womb trouble" ever since the birth of her last child, ten years ago. She had been pregnant once since that time, five years ago, but miscarried. Menstruation was regular, and of the three-day type. She consulted me. Tuly 27, 1908, and at that time had not menstruated regularly siuce the i revious November. That was eight months previous. In January she had i3assed several large clots, but nothing that resembled a fetus or placenta. The bleeding lasted two to three days. On April 6th there was a return of bleeding for part of one day. On Jul 6th there began a bloody discharge which persisted until the time of her tirst consultation. Two weeks previously pains in both sides of the lower abdomen began to be felt. Severe backache. The total quantity of blood lost was inconsiderable.

Examination showed the cervix somewhat softened and closed; the uterus approximately the size of a clenched tist, semi solid in consistency. It was too hard for a pregnant, too soft for a normal, uterus. The diagnosis of missed abortion was made and the patient advised to enter the hospital to have the uterus emptied. She entered July 31st. An ice-cap was applied to the abdomen for the relief of pain. Since expulsion of the uterine contents did not follow tamponade, and the temperature rose to 100 degrees, it was decided on August 3d to give an anesthetic and remove the uterine contents digitally. The cervix was gradually dilated by the finger until it could be inserted far enough for the second joint of the finger to be beyond the internal os. Then a hard globular mass the size of a large English walnut could be felt in the left horn, closely attached to the uterine wall. When this was freed and an attempt was made to crush it sufficiently to pull it out of the uterine cavity, difficulty was encountered. "What was left of the ovum was almost as hard as a fibroid, and on pressure it slipped around in the uterine cavity as a pool ball might in its pocket. The finger was withdrawn and the placenta crushed by an ovum forceps; the smaller pieces could then be readily extracted. Final revision by the finger showed that the uterine cavity was now completely emi3tied. I was particularly struck with the pocket left by the long-retained placenta. The uterine muscle did not contract down at once as it does ordinarily. Nevertheless the bleeding was only moderate. A curettement followed placental removal.

The day following digital removal the patient's temperature rose to 10111; degrees, pulse 100, but fell to normal on the second day and remained so. There was no subsequent inflammatory trouble, but a rather prolonged blood-tinged discharge due to the slow involution of the uterus. Eecovery was, however, complete.

Wlicii; ijX we to speak of a placenta as being retained? Ordinarily if it still remains in tlic uterus after six to twelve hours, the term "retained j)lacenta" is used. Where we have such a "retained placenta," writers are by no moans agreed as to the correct time for operative interference. Moebius recommends innnediately em)ty-ing the uterus. Boldt i))-efers to wait for twenty-four hours before resorting to 0)erative measures. Where there is no fever or lioiiiorrhage, and only a small portion of placental tissue has been Ietaiued, one can safely wait from twenty-four to forty-eight hours. Should the entire i)lacenta or a greater portion of it be left in the uterus, do not wait longer than twenty-four hours for spontaneous expulsion.

So much for the length of time one should wait before adopting opeiative measures. The nature of these operative measures will dejjend primarily upon the stage of tlie pregnancy and the dilatation of the cervix.

If the abortion has occurred some time within the first six weeks of gestation and the whole or a part of the placenta is retained, we must first examine digitally to see how much is still left in utcro. If the amount is considerable, digital removal should be resorted to, but if the amount is small, the dull or sharp curette will remove it entirely with the least pain to the patient.

Case No. 13. Mrs. R. J. O., 23 years, had had two children, the last one in November, 1906. She came to see me on June 9, 1908, with tlie following history: Since her last childbirth she had been pregnant four times, but on each occasion had procured criminal abortion by a midwife. The last miscarriage, five weeks previous to this consultation, had progressed to three and one-half months. Since then there had been backache, bloody discharge and occasional abdominal pains. The uterus was somewhat enlarged and soft. Since ergot, hot douches and rest failed to relieve her, a curettement was resorted to in July. A few small pieces of placental tissue and much thickened endometrium were scraped away. Recovery was prompt.

In abortions between the sixth and twelfth week retention of the placenta had best be treated by "curage" or digital removal unless the intra-uterine tampon is sufficient to accomplish the purpose.

RETAINED PLACENTA.

Abortiwus rroiu the Iweulh to tlio twenty juurtli week, wliere the placenta has been retained, must be handled with special care. Digital removal in many of these cases is only possible where tivo iiugcrs can be introduced into the uterus. A considerable dilatation of the cervix is necessary for this purpose. Kleinwaechter therefore advises the preliminary use of the tampon in all these cases so that the lingers may be quickly slipped into the uterus and the placenta Ic-inoved. At times it is necessary on account of nnnsnal adherence to use the curette for the removal of particles of tissue, always, however, under the guidance of the finger. "Ward advises against a curettage after the twelfth week. ITe prefers to tampon and wait a while longer if there is no immediate indication for interference, such as fever or hemorrhage. In general, tlierefore, we can summarize the treatment as in the nc(oni innying table ()age 131).

Sepsis

The most serious danger of abortion is sapremia and septic infection. Occasionally it is only a mild, transient affair; at other times it is so virulent as either to cause the woman's death or make her an invalid for life.

The frequency of sepsis in these cases is due to (1) Tlie lack of cleanliness on the part of the patient and doctor.

(2) The large proportion of instrumental abortions.

(3) The frequency of retained placenta.

Sapremia. Fever is constantly present in these cases, but it. will vary greatly in degree, and there will likewise be a great difference in the extent of the toxemia present in each case. P ortnnately the greater number of these cases are of a sapremic nature. We have an elevation of temperature to 100 to 101, slight chilly sensations, a pulse of 90 to 100, a foul-smelling bloody discharge and occasionally cramp-like pains. The natural assumption with such symptoms should be that some portions of the ovum have been retained and that the absorption from the necrotic masses in the uterus is responsible for the fever. The treatment consists, first of all, in the use of an intrauterine tampon for twelve hours. If this does not result in the expulsion of the retained material, we should employ digital removal, followed ordinarily by an antiseptic intrauterine douche. Iany advise not waiting for the results of a tamponade in cases of elevation of temperature, but proceeding at once with digital removal and douche. The feeling in favor of immediate removal is influenced by the knowledge that with an open cervix and a necrotic retained placenta the danger of serious infection is too great to iermit of any delay. After removal and douche have been completed, it is not rare for the patient to have a chill and a rise of temjieratnre to 103 or even as high as 105 to 10(5. This. need not cnusi; il; irni unless tlic tcmiikTiiturc Iciiiaiiis nhove 101 nw llic Ioluiwiiii; day. (i-ilinarily tlicic is a rapid Iall in temperature, reaching normal on Ihc evening ol Ilic second day. The higli fever is due to partial absorption ol toxic material from the necrotic placenta loosened liy tlie digital nianii)ulations. ()(ca sionally such a sapremia will rc(juire a second intrautcilnc dourhc to vasli away the smaller debris still lell in llie uterus. If the temperature remains high, the cause is usually a true septic infection.

Sepsis. The true septic infections due to yogeinc micro-organ isms ruu a very dilierent course and may generally bt considered as either of a mild or severe character.

Considering the large percentage of abortions that are due to instrumental interference (criminal), and considering above all the careless, nay even unclean, way in which such instrumentation is usually done, it is amazing thai the number of serious infections is not greater than it is. The number of lives lost annually by septic abortions is ditficult to estimate, since the facts in tlie. se cases are usually concealed, but it would doubtless be found to be appallingly large. (See (hai)ter 1 II.)

Mild Form. The treatment of se itic abortion must depend in the main on the severity of the infection. In the milder cases we usually have a fever of 103 to loSV. degrees, a pulse of 120, rigors, some toxemia and considerable pain in the lower abdomen. The first object must be to find out whether the fever is clue merely to an infection or whether, beside this, portions of the ovum are retained. The patient's history will usually give some clew to this question. If the bloody discharge has a foul odor it points to retained placenta. The size of the uterus will indicate whether or not everything has been expelled. The true condition can only be positivelj determined by digital exploration of the uterine cavity, but, since, in these infected cases, this is both painful and dangerous, it is not usually done imless there is good reason to suspect placental retention. If larger pieces are Ietained, they should be removed at the time of this examination. If the retained pieces are smaller, it is better in these eases of infection to use a dull curette or a placental foiceps under the guidance of the finger. Of the two the large dull curette or the spoon curette of Orthmann is probably a safer instrument than the placental forceps, since the latter may, in the event of a perforation, cause fatal injuries. Having determined by digital exploration just where the phiceiital pieces are attaclied, the curette is gently passed upwaid to that region and without using any pressure against the wall, it is hooked over the little irregularities and partly withdrawn till they have been freed from their attachment; then they may be gently expressed by Budiu's method (Fig. 35) or caught near the internal os with a placental forceps.

In these infected cases we must above all avoid undue manipulations, since rough traction and pressure may force some of the material into the neighboring lymphatics and so cause the disease to get beyond the limits of the uterine mucosa. A n y thin g that causes the formation of new wound spaces, such as the use of the sharp curette or forcible cervical dilatation, is bound to increase the possibility of spreading infection.

Where the uterus is emiity, the majority of operators prefer simply to give antiseptic douches. At the start one or two intrauterine douches can be given with a one-half)er cent lysol or 1 to 6,000 bichloride solution. Stronger solutions of bichloride should be avoided, as the absorption from a recently pregnant uterus is so rapid that serious intoxications may result. If the temperature drops to normal or does not rise over 101 we nmy content ourselves in the further management by giving merely vaginal douches. An ice-cai) o the abdomen will relieve the pain and diminish any inflammatory process about the uterus. Internally we can give whisky and quinine in moderate doses, depending on the special indications. Should the fever still persist over 102.5 we must be on the lookout for trouble beyond the limits of the uteius. This temperature may be due to suppurative trouble in the tube, the ovary or the pelvic cellular tissue. Where the suppuration occurs in the peritoneal cavity the fever is usually higher (105) and the general toxemia more prominent. Suppurative processes thus localized may take the form either of diffuse cellular exudates or of abscess formation. In the former event we may continue with conservative methods of absorption (douches, sedatives, ice-caps), but where there is distinct fluctuation of a larger mass, we must in the face of a persistent fever make a vaginal incision to let out the pus, and drain.

Gonorrhoea! infections give a much more favorable prognosis. The character of the uterine discharge (yellow, glairy) and the presence of gonococci in the stained smear will establish the diagnosis.

lu sucli pnt-ients we sliuuld try absorptive treatment much longer than where streptococci or stapliylococci are found.

Severe Form. Tlie minU-r cases of infection may at any time, from one cause or another, assume a more virulent form; and in certain individuals the disease may begin at once with alarming symptoms. Such women after a hard chill have a fever reaching 104 to 106. The temperature runs an irregiilar course; there aie sharp declines and equalh sudden elevations, with sweats, great prostration, rapid jiulse, intense abdominal pain, and some tympanites; in other words, the classical picture of a rapidly spreading septic process. Here, rest is the essential. Unless larger pieces of placenta have been retained, digital removal with its necessarily violent manipulations should not be resorted to. The large blunt curette, with perhaps the assistance of ecouvillouuage as described in Chapter XVII, will suffice to clean out the shieds still left in the uterus. One intra-uterine douche should be given, but, if the general condition of the patient is not good, as much would be lost as gained by repeatedly disturbing her in this way. These patients are apt to be over-treated. It is difficult to decide in a given case just what plan to pursue.

General Measures. Best in bed is most essential in all these cases. The patient should be kept in one position all the time, unless the discomfort of such absolute quiet is too intolei-able. The proper sort of bed will help greatly in the treatment. Air-cushions or air-rings will to a considerable extent prevent pressure on the patient's hips. Best of all is the so-called water bed, but this will usually not be obtainable except at hospitals.

Attention to hygiene of the mouth will do much to keep up the patient's general strength. The teeth should be brushed daily with some mild antiseptic solution. Parched lips can be soothed by applications of a bit of gauze moistened with glycerine. If the temperature runs over 102.5, the extremities, face and chest should be sponged with cold water or alcohol. Headache can be relieved with an ice-cap. This is much better than cold moist cloths that wet the hair and pillow.

For sleeplessness, where there is no severe pain, it is best to prescribe veronal in doses of live to twelve grains. If the fever is persistent, it is preferable to employ laetophenin in a dosage of ten to fifteen grains. Pain is, however, best relieved by opiates, which at the same time produce sleep. For the relief of the muscular and nerve pains, aspirin grs. v, novaspirin grs. x, or p Tamidon grs. v, maj be employed.

Local Measures. The effort to combat septic infection by local measures has been successful only to a limited degree. These local measures consist of (1) Vaginal douches.

(2) Intra-uterine douches.

(3) Local applications.
(4) Continuous intra-uterine irrigation.
(5) Tamponade.
(6) Vaporization.

Figure 53 Position of patient for giving a vaginal douche. In giving an intra-uterine douche the genitals must always be thoroughly cleansed and well exposed before introducing the nozzle under the guidance of the finger. (Crossen.)

The: v i)tal douche is the least dangerous of these measures and shouhl he employed in the majority oi eases, it serves to wash away the collected lochia! How ivdiii the vagiua, stimulates the uterus to contraction, relieves pain and to some extent diicctly reduces inflammation. on Ilerfi strongly i-econnuends 1 to 5,000 bichloride or 1 to 200 permanganate for siuh douches. Douches can be given two to three times a day, but if more seem necessary, for one reason or another, it is advisable to alternate in the antisei)ti employed in the douche to avoid poisoning. In anemia or diseases of tlic heart or kidneys, bichloride should not be used.

Intrantcrine douches should always be given iuunediately after a curettage or other intrauterine manijiulatious. If there is a marked drop in the fever after such a douche and the fever should again rise, it may be repeated once. But if two oi- three such douches have not accomplished their pur)ose, additional ones will be useless and will even to a considerable extent prove harmful, since all these manipulations tend to open new wounds and disturb the patient's quiet. Whenever the septic process has spiead beyond the limits of the uterus, intrauteiine douches are contraindicated. On the other hand, where the process is limited to the uterine mucosa, vaginal douches, together with ergotin internally, is usually all that is necessary.

Local applications to tears about the cervix or vagina are indicated only in those patients in whom the disease is practically localized to these wound surfaces. Tincture of iodine or twent per cent, silver nitrate are the safest and most effective antiseptic cauterauts to employ. The infected wounds must be accurately exposed with specula so that the medicine may be applied directly to the affected area. Where clean granulations are already forming it is needless to apply such remedies.

Continuous irrigation of the uterus has been recommended by some, but has not met with much favor. The main objections are the excessive discomfort it causes the patient, the danger of poisoning by prolonged use of antiseptics, and the danger of perforation by misplacement of the uterine catheter.

Tamponade of the uterus with iodoform gauze is attended with risk of iodoform poisoning. This form of treatment, according to Von Herff, is ineffective, since bacteria have lieen found to multiply rapidly in the meshes of the gauze. Chinosol gauze has been recommended as less dangerous.

Iaporisatioii has been enthusiasticalh recommended in the treatment of uterine sepsis by its originator, Dr. Pincus. It consists of the applications of siij erheated steam by means of a special apparatus to the entire uterine cavity, thus killing all bacteria and causing necrosis of the uterine mucosa. Several serious accidents have shown this method to be a dangerous and inefficient one, and in consequence it has generally been abandoned.

Among the methods for increasing the body resistance to septic invasion, the best is the production of active hyperemia. Passive hyperemia is, at least at the present time, a technical impossibility. We have no apparatus or other method that will bring about such a passive congestion in the pelvis. Only the cervix is in a limited way amenable to this form of treatment. The best method of obtaining active pelvic hyperemia is the ai plication of drj or moist heat to the abdomen. Extreme cold acts somewhat like extreme heat, but its effect is a more superficial one. It is, however, a question whether these measures are of real benefit in increasing body resistance and whether the good results are not mainly due to the relief of the associated pain. Heat or cold can be applied in accordance with the individual susceptibility of the patient. Some tolerate the one better, some the other. In one class of cases, however, heat, particularly if applied in the form of dry heat at 120 to 150 centigrade, causes decided benefit. These are the subacute inflammations of the cellular tissue, the plastic exudates left after the acute septic process has subsided. Here a very rapid improvement is noticed if the patient's abdomen and pelvis are placed in an electric light bath for ten to thirty minutes every other day. The apparatus as described by Polano (Fig. 54) can, however, hardly be used outside of a hospital, since it is too bulky to carry around. The temperature within the asbestos-lined case can be regulated by the number of electric lights turned on. Dry heat can be tolerated much more readily than moist heat.

Heat, as ordinarily applied for the relief of pain and acute pelvic inflammation can be used in either the dry or moist form. The thermophore bags are serviceable and the little Japanese stove when used in conjunction with a hot poultice will help the latter to retain its temperature for a much longer time than would otherwise be Iiii: i: ATIuX A- U TUEATMKNT Ul ABOUL'ION.

possil)lc. One lliiiia; to romenibor is tliat in sueli aciito localized peri-touitis till iiatient will tolcialc V(My little weii lit on the abdomen.

Injections into the blood. The destruction of the bacteria in the blood nr liody tissues has been attempted by the injection of various antiseptic solutions, but experiments made thus far show that this is associated with considerable danger and veiy questionable benefit. Formaldehyde has thus been injected in strengths of 1 to 5,000 or (nen 1 to 1,500. Results are not much better with the injection of special blood sera. 11 the so-called streptococcus anti-

Figure 54 Treatment of pelvic cellulitis by means of Polano's hot-air bath. The heat is produced by electric lights. The asbestos cover is in two parts and extensible so as to embrace as much of the body as is desired. A very high degree of dry heat is tolerated by this method. (Gellhorn.) toxins thus far manufactured have proven ineffective in the majority of cases. This is doubtless due in great part to the fact that the immune amboceptors of the horse do not fit in with the complement of human blood. The blood sera can only help if tliey are injected early in the spread of a bacteriemia. In localized septic conditions they cannot be of any assistance. The injection of larger amounts of serum does harm rather than good, since there results an excess of certain dangerous substances in the blood. Clinically some apparently wonderful cures have been reported by the injection of these antitoxins, but when closely analyzed it will be seen that only a small percentage of them are really due to the antitoxin. Axonson's or Marmorek's serum is especially reliable. Of these, 500 to 2,000 units should be injected on the fourth day and repeated on the sixth. No more should be given.

Among the substances occasionally injected into the blood for the relief of these septic conditions there must still be considered tjie preparations of silver in colloid solution. These apparently act not directly by killing the bacteria in the blood, but rather by interfering with their growth and by acting upon the toxins and other end-products of bacterial change in such a way as to render them less poisonous. They also cause an increased phagocytosis. The most commonly used of these silver preparations is Collargolum, which is used in intravenous injections of a five per cent, solution in water. After due sterilization of the solution, the instruments and the site of injection, three to nine c. c. are injected into the median vein of the arm. It. is well to inject the substance veiy slowly, that is to say, fifteen to twenty drops at a time. If the point of the needle slips to one side of the vein, and the injection is made into the tissues, it causes considerable pain. If no improvement has taken place in twelve hours, the injection is to be repeated and twice daily thereafter. Where the effect is immediately beneficial, the injections need only be given every twenty-four to forty-eight hours. It should be added, however, that many careful observers deny any therapeutic value to Collargolum. The use of silver in the form of inunctions such as the well-known "Unguentum Crede" has been shown to be of practically no benefit, since so little of the silver is absorbed into the system in that way.

Finally, a word as to the use of alcohol in sepsis. It was at one time our most popular weapon, but more and more we have come to realize that its dangeis are numerous, that it probably does a great deal more harm than good, since its temporary stimulation is followed by a period of depression. The elimination of toxins from the kidneys is interfered with, the heart muscle weakened, the digestive powers of stomach and intestines diminished. So it had best be given only exceptionally for temporary stimulation.

Operative Treatment. There will not be space to consider at length the various operative procedures necessary in the treatment of these septic conditions. One of them has already been mentioned curettage. It is a most dangerous procedure and should never be rni; Kxriox and tukatmiai or ahoktiox.

eiii)loyo(l, oxfojit after very early iiiiscairiages where the chance for a sect)n(lary pyemia is slight. A curettage is of course contra-indicated in serious infection outside the uterus.

Wlicrcver there is a fluctuating mass indicative of suppuration in tlio pelvic cavity, and tlie continued fever and pain show tliat tlic process is not receding, the pus should he evacuated. This is pref erably done tlirough the vagina, but at times, if the abscess lies liigji u) lieyond the reach of aiiiiial iiislruincnts. the incision will liave

Figure 55 Fowler position assumed in j eptic cases after tlie pus has been evacuated from the pelvis by a drainage incision. (Crossen.) to be made through the abdomen or along the groin. It is best not to remove the inflamed tube and ovaries, but simjily to incise and drain. If the fever and toxemia associated with the abscess is moderate, this rule may be broken and tube and ovary, if extensively involved, should be removed. Many of these milder cases are gonorrhoea! pus-tubes due to the spread of a cervical infection through the manipulations attendant on the miscarriage. The quicker the operator gets through his operation, the better for the patient. In the weakened condition of these women, ten or fifteen minutes more means a good deal.

Tlie ligation of septic thrombi lying in the pelvic veins, as advised by Bnnnn. has received considerable stndy lately and doubtless will occasionally save a liie, but the selection of the cases in which such an operation is indicated is a matter of such extreme difiiculty that except in large clinics it had better not be employed. Hysterectomy is also recommended for certain of these septic eases, but with much less enthusiasm than formerly. Still, if done in time, before the sepsis has spread beyond the uterus in cases of severe local infection, results are good. It is best to do the operation as a supra-vaginal abdominal am)utation of the uterus, since in this way there is the least danger of infecting the peritoneum or cellular tissue with the septic lochial discharge.

The rather conservative stand taken relative to the treatment of septic cases has just recently (June. 1909) received further confirmation at the meeting of the German Gynecological Society at Strafshurg, where this subject was one of the main topics of discussion.

Perforation 111 110 coinplicatiou of aboilioii can a mistake in. iudniiient or techiiique ou the part of the practitioner lead to more serious results than in accidental iserforation of the uterus. Perforation is one of those misad ntures that ir(il. ihly dccur very much more Irimpiently than the printed records would indicate. Most of the eases are never reported because, after all, it is usually the operator's fault, and not a pleasant thing to write about. That Heineck was able to find record of but 160 cases of perforation in the literature of the past twelve years is no evidence of the rarity of this accident. You can hardly find a busj gynecologist who will not, when questioned, relate to you at least one such disagreeable experience. And how much more frequent must the accident be among the rank and file of i ractitioners, unaccustomed for the most part to the use of instruments and taught for many years that "abortions ought to be curetted."

Great is the variety of instruments that have i roduced perforation. In the hands of the patient herself, knitting needles, hat-pins, sounds and other instruments of criminal abortion have done so. In the hands of the accoucheur, the curette, douche-nozzle and the abortion forceps head the list. Even the finger has been responsible for a certain number of perforations. Depending upon which instrument caused the accident, and the manner in which it was used, the prognosis and treatment varies greatly. If the wound was made by a sound, or, say, a round Hegar cervical dilator, under aseptic conditions, there will be hardly any danger whatever, and there is no special cause for alarm or active treatment. While working in the clinic of a noted European gynecologist, I saw him perforate a uterus with Hegar dilators three times. Fearing the possibility of hemorrhage, he did a vaginal celiotomy, only to find three small bruised spots in the fundus as the sole consequence of the perforation. Where the perforation is made with a looped or cutting instrument like the curette, the danger is much greater. The loop of the bluut curette may catch iii a bit oi omeutum or a loop of in-testiue, and carry these structures through the)erforation opeuiug dowu into the uterus, and thence to the vagina. The sharp curette lias the additional disadvantage that it may tear a hole through the intestine or seriously bruise and cut the parietal and visceral peritoneum. When carelessly used, the most dangerous instrument is the ovum forceps. Its correct manipulation has been described in the chapter on Operative Technique. If it is employed blindly to loosen and grasp pieces of adherent placental tissue, it will, as likely as not, perforate the uterus and clamp down upon a loop of intestine. In the case reported by Hartmann, some fifteen inches of rectal and sigmoidal mucous membrane were pulled out and cut off before it was noticed that a mistake had been made. We may divide perforations into (1) Simple perforations.

(2) Perforation with prolapse of omentum.

(3) Perforation with prolapse of intestines.

Naturally the simple perforation without injury to abdominal structures will be the most numerous, and attended with least danger to the patient. If the uterus is free from infectious bacteria and the instnmientatiou done in an aseptic manner, the possibility of causing serious trouble by such a perforation of the uterus is comparatively small. AVhere, however, there has been a uterine infection, a penetration of the uterine wall by means of an instrument is apt to set up a dangerous, often fatal, peritonitis.

The larger the perforation opening, the greater is the likelihood of the prolapse of some of the abdominal contents through this opening. The omentum has in a number of instances thus been pulled out into the vagina. Where the mistake was noticed at once, the omentum replaced, and the uterine cavity packed with gauze, the outcome was, as a rule, not fatal.

Prolapse of the intestines through the perforation wound in the uterus is a more dangerous complication. Something is grasped blindly and pulled upon. To the inexperienced it looks like a membrane. It is pulled out and cut off. In several instances a foot or more of intestine was thus removed before the mistake was discovered. Death is the universal outcome of this error unless the patient is immediately operated on.

Mciitioji lias been iiiadi dl tlic oxuni forceps as a rn(U(iit raiiso (it ikrfuration. Doubtless it is tlic most dangerous of tiie various instruments used because it grasps, pulls down and crushes llie tissues tliat lie in its iatli, whereas the bluut curette and sound merelj cause superlicial injury. J'lie St. Cyr auger curette was responsible for several eases in the tabulation made by Ileineck. Plie catheter and uterine irrigator have been known to cause perforation, as well as many other instruments used for mrposes of abortion.

The linger,-which is the most sensitive and most readily controlled of the means for em)tying the uterus, is not exemjit from blame in this connection. A number of cases are now on record in which the linger pressed through the uterine wall without the operator's detecting the mistake ami brought down some of the abdominal structures, nsually the ouieutnm. Fortunatelv, the tiuger is not so apt to cause direct trauuui to these structures, so that if they are at once replaced, and no infection has been present, recovery is the rule. Owing to the fact that the curette is still the favorite means o f e y a c u a t i n g the u t e r i n e c a v i t y after abortion, this instrument is the most frequent cause of uterine perforation. In lieineck's table there was i"ecord of forty-one such cases. The perforation may be in the cervix uteri or in the corpus, or may involve both cervix and corpus. The size and number of the perforations varies greatly. In Werelins' case there were seven punctures.

Symptoms. The symptoms of perforation are those of the associated internal hemorrhage, shock, or i)eritonitis. There is usually marked collapse whenever the abdominal organs have l)een much contused. The hemorrhage may come from the tear in the uterine wall or from injury to some of the abdominal viscera. Peritonitis results either from infection carried from the uterine cavity into the peritoneal cavity, or from injury to the intestines attended by the escape of intestinal contents.

Diagnosis. "While it is not always possible to prevent a peifora-tion, the physician is certainly at fault if he fails to recognize his mistake when it has been made. Any one at all familiar with anatomy should be able to differentiate omentum and intestines from placenta and membranes. Likewise, if he has been careful enovrgh to estimate the size of the uterus by bimanual examination, he should be able to tell, when his curette or dilator slips in too far, that he has caused a perforatiou. lu one set of cases, however, the diagnosis of perforation may be made incorrectly. These are the instances of so-called paralysis of the uterine muscle. AVe know that in certain individuals there may be a marked relaxation of the in voluntary muscle fibers of the uterus, similar to the condition in acute dilatation of the stomach. The walls of such a uterus will yield to the instnmient, allowing it to slip in so far as to suggest a perforation. Van Tussenbroek has taken a very decided stand in

Figure 56 Bicornuate pregnant uterus, presenting conditions almost identical to those in Case 14. (Kelly.) the argument on this point favoring the possibility of such a relaxation, and citing numerous cases in defense of her aigument. Doubtless such a relaxation does at times occur, but it must surely be a very rare phenomenon, and perforation will in the majority of cases prove to be the correct diagnosis.

Another point of differentiation is the bicornuate uterus with pregnancy in one horn. If an abortion occi rs in such a uterus it may happen that the sound introduced to measure the cavity is passed into the smaller non- iregnant half of the uterus, and that when later the blunt curette is used to empty the uterus it goes into the pregnant half and enters so mucli further that the diagnosis of a perforation seems almost certain.

Case No. 14. The iouowiug interesting case occurred iu tlie winter of 1899 during my service at the City Female Hospital. For a period of three months previous to entering the hospital, the patient had ol)served an intermittent slight bloody discharge in place of her regular menstruation. There were nausea and other symptoms of pregnancy. Digital examination revealed a firm pear-shaped l)o(ly to the left corresponding in size to the slightly enlarged uterus. To Uic right lay a nuctuating tuiikir the size of a pineapple, closely adherent to tlie uterus, sliglitly sensitive. No symptoms of shock or fever. The diagnosis lay between ovarian cj st with an early aborting uterus on the one hand and unruptured right-sided ectopic pregnancy on the other. The careful introduction of a sound corroborated the presence of the uterine body on the left; it entered to a doplli of three and a half inches. A diagnostic curettement was advised. The report of the assistant who did the curettement was that when he introduced the curette to obtain enough material for examination, it passed unobstructed to a depth of over six inches. At the same time there was a profuse hemorrhage. He felt certain he had perforated the uterus, and, packing the uterus and cervix with gauze, he stopped all further manipulations. Twenty-four hours later, when the gauze was removed, a somewhat lacerated fetus and placenta were found lying in the vagina. The patient remained in excellent condition. Subsequent exploration revealed the presence of a septum in the uterine cavity. The mass to the right was, therefore, a pregnancy in the right horn of a bicornuate uterus. Recovery was complete.

Finally, a sound may pass along the Fallopian tubes from the uterine cavity in certain rare instances where the isthmus tubae is patulous, and thus produce the impression of a uterine perforation. The diagnosis can here be made by the direction of the sound, and by the limited range of mobility. Doubtless these cases of tubal sounding are mneli rarer tlian was formerly thought to be the case.

Cause and Prevention. The prophylaxis of perforation is so intimately associated with the cause that I have preferred to consider them together.

Augustin has assigned three main causes for uterine pei"-f oration: (1) The pathologic condition of the uterus.

(2) The use of dangerous iustrumeuts.

(3) Faulty technique.

To these three, Orthmann adds a fourth: (4) Insuflicient or careless examiuation of local condition.

(1) The uterine wall may at times be as soft as butter and offer no resistance whatever to instrumentation. This is especially true where there has been inflammatory trouble of the pelvic organs. Kuntzsch cites several cases where the contributing cause of the perforation was the abnormal softness of the uterine wall. Where the abortion is complicated with libroid, the wall of the uterus is often abnormally thin and friable in certain portions.

(2) The dangerous instruments that are responsible for perforation have already been mentioned. The main point is that all instruments used for emptying the aborting uterus should be blunt. This applies particularly to the curette and to the ovum forceps. There have been devised many varieties of ovum forceps. One of the best is Winter's, which is a modification of the original type of Pchultze. These consist of a pair of forceps, whose ends are larger than normal, blunt and scooped out so that they can contain some of the material loosened from the uterine wall. Schulze's instrument had sharp edges, which in Winter's were rounded off so as to decrease the danger of pinching off uterine tissue. Nassauer modified the instrument so as to prevent any tight closuie of the two blades and thereby preclude the possibility of pinching off a piece of uterine wall, intestine, etc. In this coimtry, too, there are in use a great variety of ovum forceps, many of which are dangerous.

(3) Faulty technique is probably the chief cause of perforation. Gentleness must mark all the manipulations about the pregnant uterus. Rough, quick work is bound to result in injury. Only by the selection of the proper instrument can wp hope to eliminate these cases of perforation. To use a curette in a uterus of five months' gestation is nothing short of criminal carelessness, and yet in actual practice this occurs with moderate frequency. A point in technique concerning which there has been much discussion, is whether counter-pressure from above when ovum forceps were employed did not predispose to perforation. On the one hand, it definitely locates tlio size and position (if till utci-us. and yet. on llic dtlui', as Ilallian's case would indicatf. it, nives () i i(iilnnity Ior a piece of uterine wall to l)e l)iiklieil between the hlades of the ovum forceps. Auother mistake in teolinii ue that may prove dangerons is to intvodnee a closed forceps deeply into the uterine cavity, and then open it. If the

forceps has partly penetrated the uterine wall, such a proceduri will result in tearing open a hole in the wall at this point. The forceps should be opened as soon as it gets beyoutl the internal os. There can be no (piestion that the finger is far safer than any instrument in the removal of material ivom the uterus.

faulty techni(ue can also occui in the dilatation of the cervix l)r(liniinaiy to enqitying tiie uterus. If Hegar's graduated lila tors are used, care must be taken to measure the depth of the uterine cavity i)reviously, so that each dilator is introduced only far enough to i ass beyond the internal os. If special care is not observed in this regard, perforation may readily occur. It is best to measure off the exact distance with the finger upon each instrument before it is introduced. The finger tlms placed as a constant guide will be a warning not to introduce the dilator too deeply (Fig. 39), Branched dilators, if used briskly, may give rise to perforation in the region of the cervix. Unless there is need for special haste, it is better to use the tampon or the inelastic bag dilator of Voorhees or Champetier-de-Ribes, especially if the pregnancy has developed over six weeks or two months.

Treatment. The treatment of perforation will de)end u ion four factors: (1) the size and number of the perforations; (2) the septic condition of the uterus or instruments; (3) the injuries to other organs beside the uterus; (4) hemorrhage. Where the opening in the uterus is not large, the uterus and instrument apparently clean, and there is no evident injury to other structures, it is best to keep the patient absolutely (uiet for at least three days, and await developments. The presence of an internal hemorrhage will indicate a lapaiotomy. The hemorrhage can be checked by suturing the hole in the uterus, or, if that organ be much damaged, by hysterectomy. Septic cases should be drained. Whenever there is a likelihood of sepsis associated with the perforation it is best to remove the uterus. Wherever the omentum or intestines have been dragged through the perforation wound and the extent of the visceral injuries is undetermined, it is advisable to open the abdomen at once and do such necessary repair of injuries as is possible to be done without too much shock to the patient. Some cases have been reported in which twelve feet or more of the intestines had to be resected.

Naturally, a peiforated uterus should never be swabbed with caustics nor irrigated with any solutions. Doubtless subsequent irrigation is one of the most frequent causes of death after uterine perforation. The absorptive power of the peritoneum is great, and cases of severe mercurial poisoning have been reported. Above all, as far as the jdractitioner is concerned, the thing to do is to recognize the fact that a perforation has occurred and to stop at once all instrumentation. If the uteriue contents have not been emptied, this should be done with the finger as gently as possible, or, as Heineck has suggested, it may be done with a curette, while the uterus is being watched from above through a laparotomy incision.

These cases of perforation, whenever complicated so as to require operative measures, should be taken to a hospital at once. There is almost invariably some morbidity so that the patients require careful nursing afterwards.

Missed Abortion

Uuusiuil irritability oi the uterine musele lias been meutioued as one of the predisposing causes of abortion. At times the opposite extreme is found, namely, a markedly lessened sensibility of the uterus. In the event of tlie death of the fetus, this lessened

THE PREVENTION AND TREATMENT OF ABORTION 77

sensibility may under certain circumstances lead to a retention of the ovum for many weeks, or even months. In sucli cases we speak of "missed" or "delayed" abortion. The term was first employed by J. j l. Duncan, the eminent Scotch obstetrician, in 1880.

8ucli a long retained ovum dill'ers in many respects from the normal ovum of the same i)eriod of development. The placenta is usually hard and scirrhus, is pear-shaped, and has a yellowish white color. Here and there a small subchorionic hemorrhage can be seen, but these hemorrhages do not equal in extent or number those that we find in the hematoma-mole. Upon the serotinal surface there are a few dry sinewy areas. The amniotic cavity is much reduced in size and only a small cjuantity of amniotic fluid left. The embryo usually shows degenerative changes similar to those in mole pregnancy. There may be partial mummification in fetuses from the third to the sixth month.

Microscopically we usually find the decidua well preserved in spite of the fact that the ovum has been retained many months. In ova of the first few months there may even occur some decidual proliferation. The chorionic epithelium is also but little affected by the impaired nutrition of prolonged retention. This epithelium is primarily nourished by the blood in the intervillous spaces and as long as these spaces are not blocked by thrombotic processes, syncytium and Langhans' cells are well preserved. The chorionic connective tissue, on the contrary, becomes oedematous and here and there undergoes coagulation necrosis. It never proliferates after the death of the fetus, but rather shows retrogressive changes. The fetal blood vessels are completely obliteiated and many maternal vessels show thrombosis with uecrobiosis of the sunoundiiig deeidua. The longer the ovum is retained, the more often do we tiud partial regeneration of the uterine mucosa at those points where the placenta has become detached.

The cause of the retention in these cases and the cause of the final expulsion of the uterine contents must remain a mystery so long as the physiological processes involved in the expulsion of the child at full term are still so little imderstood. Graefe and Iraenkel found retention more commonly in women wlio had nursed their children an abnormally long time (twelve to twenty months). Retio-flexiou of the uterus is given as a)redis)osing factn by Graefe. Prolonged rest in bed might cause a delay in expulsion, and apparently this influenced the retention in one of my cases.

The history of a missed abortion is usually as follows: There is a cessation of menstruation for three or four months, then a slight bloody discharge associated with some uterine cramps. At this

Figure 57 Hyjiamnios ovum, in which the emljimi was S mms. long ami the ovum 9 cms. long. (Case 15.) E = Embryo.

time the fetus dies, but is retained. For months afterwards, sometimes for as long as a year, there may be a discharge tinged with blood and occasional cramp-like pains. The iiterus does not increase in size as the patient e. xpects, but, on the contrary, there is usually some decrease in its size. Finally pains set in inore vigorously and the ovum is expelled. Fever and iii. ircrjitioii are ordinarily absent. The following case well illustrates this clinical course:

Case No'. 15. M, W., twenty-three years of age, bad been married live years. No pievious pregnancy. For several years bad leucor-rboea, backacbe and dragging pains in the pelvis. Menses regular, three or four days in duiation, painless. Last menstruation in the middle of September. In October had typical morning sickness. No symptoms on the part of the breasts. "When she came to me on February 11th, she said she had had some bleeding and abdominal pains for the past week; in the past two days bleeding more severe, and accompanied by clots. Examination showed a uterus somewhat softened, corresponding in size, however, only to about a two montlis' pregnancy. She was ordered to rest in bed and given sedatives, but the following day, five montlis after the last menses, the ovum was expelled. The measurements taken before preservation showed the greatest diameter of the ovum to be 9 cm., the length of the embryo 8 mm. The placental site had not yet been established, villi being found in all portions of the ovum. The decidua was lacking in the area near the point of insertion of the umbilical cord. The embryo was well preserved, but deformed. It dated from the end of the first month. The ovum corresponded in size to two and a half months. The pregnancy continued for five months.

The diagnosis is comparatively easy if the patient has been under observation some time, but later on, when the uterus has become firmer and has lost the characteristic signs of pregnancy, the differentiation from a fibroid uterus is rather difficult. A favorable prognosis can be made, as infection, when it occurs, is limited to the uterine cavity. Severe hemorrhages are rare.

Treatment. "Where the diagnosis of missed abortion has been made with reasonable certainty, the expulsion of the ovum should be hastened, not merely because of the possibility of infection through long retention, but also because the patient is usually much distressed by the fact that she is carrying around a dead fetus in her womb. A thorough uterine and vaginal tamponade will either cause the expulsion of the ovum or result in sufficient dilatation to admit the introduction of a finger for the purpose of removing the ovum. In very rare instances it may prove necessaiy to make an incision through the cervix in order to remove the hardened placenta, the procedure resembling the vaginal enucleation of a submucous fibroid. The uterus has usually undergone partial involution and is rather firm. Hence a curettement can be done with little risk of perforation, and is advisable in all these cases. Best in bed need not be prolonged one week is enough but ergot in liberal doses for a month or six weeks should be administered in order to bring the sluggish uterus back to its normal size and condition.

Mole Pregnancy

A cousideratiuii nl ihc various kinds of iiuilc iregnancy is essential to a complete description of abortion ova. In the jirevious chapter, on retained abortion, it was seen that the ovum, although dead, might be retained in the uterus for many months afterwards. Such i-etained ova at times undergo peculiar changes, so that they lose to a great extent tlieir former characteristics, and are then called mole pregnancies. AVe can distinguish three classes of moles: (1) Fleshy or carueous moles; (2) Breus or hematoma moles; (3) Hydatid moles. In the first two instances the mole formation is essentially due to liemorrhages. In the third class of moles we are dealing with a neoplastic iiroliferation.

(1) Fleshy or Carneous Moles. For many centuries physicians have been puzzled by the occasional expulsion from the uterus of a bloody mass containing no embryo, and yet attended by man. Y of the symptoms of pregnancy. There was, indeed, much debate as to whether or not pregnancy was essential to the formation of a mole. It can readily be understood that the differentiation between a submucous fibroid and a fleshy mole must have been very difficult in former times. The fleshy mole is formed by hemorrhage infiltrating not merely the entire placental site, but also filling and thus obliterating the amniotic cavity. Naturally, these moles only form in abortion ova of the first two months of pregnancy; in more advanced pregnancies the tissues do not permit of such diffuse hemorrhagic infiltration.

For the formation of such a mole the essential factor is diminished sensitiveness to stimulation on the part of the uterine muscles. This sluggishness to irritation of one sort or another is but poorly understood and seems to vary greatly in the same individual at different times. Aftei- the death of the ovum, the amniotic fluid is absorbed, the amniotic cavity filled with blood, the embryo usually entirely liquofied or disintegrated, and the decidua becomes so infil- trated with blood as uo louger to be diftereutiated from the surrouud-ing tissue. The whole mass i resents rather the appearance of a blood clot with beginning fibrin formation, than that of a human ovum. At times we find a small cavity the size of a beau or less, lined by amnion.

Clinically such a mole cannot be differentiated from a retained abortion except for the fact that in the case of a fleshy mole the uterus is smaller and the tendenc to irregular bleeding is somewhat greater. Fleshy moles are usually retained three or four months after the death of the ovum.

(2) Breus or Hematoma Moles. While this form of mole is extremely interesting, it is not of great frequency, and consequently can only be given cursory consideration in a monograph of this sort. It is characterized by the formation of numerous polypoid or tuberous hematomata between the chorio-amnion and the decidua, or, to be more exact, in the intervillous spaces. Essential for the foi-mation of these collections of coagulated blood is a marked disproportion in size between the fetal membranes and the embryo. While in Vienna I had occasion at Wertheim 's clinic to make special investigations concerning the formation of these moles. From this study the following hypothesis seemed the most plausible:

"After the death of the fetus in the first or second month of gestation, the fetal membranes and the amniotic fluid increase in volume. Thus there arises a secondary hydramnios-ovum (Fig. 57). This growth continues ny to a certain point. The ovum is retained. The amniotic fluid is then gradually absorbed and the ovum as a whole shrinks somewhat in size. By the negative pressure thus produced, folds, or invaginations, of the membranes arise which become filled with the blood circulating in the intervillous spaces. By continued absorption of the fluid, together with a certain degree of stretching of the membranes by the blood clots, we have the formation of the hematomata. In this process the insertions of the villous stems act as fixed points. If the stems are close together a hemispherical or broad-based hematoma results; if far apart, a tuberous or polypoid hematoma."

In taking the clinical history, we usually meet with the statement that, although apparently pregnant for many months, the patient nevertheless experiences no corresponding increase in the size of the abdomen. She mav have a little backache and at times a slight bloody tinge to the discharge. In six out of eight of my cases, such a sliglit, moi"e or less persistent bleeding was noted.

Physical examination reveals a uterus enlarged to the size of a child's head, whose consistency is moderately soft, yet not so soft as in the normal!- pregnant uterus of the same size. The differential diagnosis from a myomatous uterus will therefore be difficult, and in niany cases imi ossible. The discharge has but rarely an offensive odor.

Case No. Hi. Ilic liistory of one of the cases studied by me in Vienna may serve to illustrate the clinical features of this form of mole pregnancy: Mrs. D., 25 years of age, servant, entered the hospital (Elizabeth-Spital), on A n-il 7, 1900. She had never aborted.

Figure 58 Hematoma mole. The embryo, partially disfigured, is seen in the center, attached to the large, thick placenta by a short umbilical cord. The placenta has been completely infiltrated by hematomata. E. = Embryo; C. L. = Chorion Laeve.

Two pregnancies, the last one a year ago. The last child died one week after the confinement. Menstruation did not, however, return. In October and December there was some scanty, irregular bleeding. Throughout the month previous to entering the hospital there was continuous bleeding of greater or less amount.

The uterus in April was approximately the size of a three months' gestation; cervix closed; no bleeding or pains. One week later the cervix began to dilate. On April 21 the ovum was expelled intact. Two days after the expulsion of the ovum a severe hemor-rliage set in, controlled by vaginal tamponade. The patient was discharged in good condition shortly afterwards.

The size of the ovum (Fig. 58) was 9 cms. long and 6 cms. in diameter. The embryo, on the other hand, was but 9 mms. long. The embryo, therefore, dated from about the fifth week; the ovum corresponded in size to about the third mouth, and the actual duration of the pregnancy, including the retention, was approximately ten to eleven months. The hematomata, covering almost the entire ovum, transformed it into an irregularly nodular mass.

The prognosis is good, both as to the immediate outcome and the future. The treatment consists of the evacuation of the uterine cavity. Since this form of mole pregnancy occurs primarily in cases with torpid uterine muscle a uterus, in other words, that does not readily react to stimulation we naturally have considerable difficulty in obtaining the expulsion of the mole i reguancy. Even a thorough cervical or vaginal tamponade may fail to bring this about. In such instances we will have to resort to digital and instrumental evacuation in order to empty the uterus.

Hydatid Moles. The most important and dangerous form of mole pregnancy is that ordinarily known as hydatidiform degeneration of the chorionic villi. Edgar has seen one case of this sort in about four thousand pregnancies. It may therefore be classed as a rather rare condition. Etiologically, tlie hydatid mole differs wholly from the two preceding ones. It is essentially a neoplasm and not a. degenerative change due to prolonged retention. So great was the influence of Eudolph Virchow that for two decades his interpretation of this pathological condition as a myxomatous degeneration of the chorion was generally accepted as correct. Now, thanks to the work of Marchand, we are reasonably sure that the marked proliferation of the fetal epithelium is at the root of the disease.

The condition occurs primarily during the first three or four months of pregnancy. The characteristic symptoms are: (1) Rapid increase in size of the uterus.

ruEVENTION AMI luEATMEXT OF ABORTIOX.

(2) Hemorrhage, varyiiiy in extent and duration, finally developing into a persistent sero-sanguineous discharge.

(3) A doughy or cystic consistency of the uterus, with absence of any palpable outlines of the fetus.

The positive diagnosis can of course be made at once when the woman passes some of the sago-liko bodies, oharacteristic of the cliauke in the chorionic villi. These bodies resemble small chorionic

Corpus uteri

Figure 59-Hydatid mole pregnancy in process of being expelled from the uterus. The grape-like character of the mole is well shown. (Bumm.) cysts. The patient may have considerable abdominal pain, owing to the rapid growth in size of the uterus. These hydatid moles are dangerous because of the attendant hemorrhage and spontaneous perforation of the uterine wall. Of late our attention has also been called to the fact that in about one-half of the cases there develops, as the result of such a mole, a very malignant e)ithelial tumor, called chorioma. Concerning choriomata. it need only be said in this couuectiou that metastases iu distant organs occur very early iu their development, and in such instances, the outcome is invariably fatal.

The treatment of hydatid mole consists of emptying the uterus as soon as the diagnosis is made. This can usually be readily effected by a uterine and vaginal tamponade, repeated if necessary after twenty-four to forty-eight hours. Not infrequently, some portion of the mole will be left in the uterus and will have to be removed by means of the finger or curette. It is safer not to curette such a patient immediately after the uterus has been emptied, owing to tlie great danger of perforation iu these eases. The curettement should be done, however, in all instances some two- or three weeks afterwards, if for no other reason than that we may thereby diminish the chances for malignant degeneration of retained material.

Therapeutic Abortion

Therapeutic abortion has been defined as the induction of abortion on the part of the physician in order to save the life of the mother. " Fhat this should be done only after consultation with another physician, and after having carefully considered the dangers by which the mother is beset, is self-evident. The subject cannot here be considered in detail, but the essential facts must be emphasized, since it is only too frequently seen that operative indications are not understood, and that we have on the one hand too much haste in i:)roduciug the abortion, and on the otlicr hand too great delay before resorting to an evacuation of the uterus.

In considering the induction of premature labor in the eighth or ninth month of pregnancy we are accustomed to speak of absolute indications and relative indications. Such a division cannot be made for the induction of abortion. In abortion, after all, conditions are quite different, for here the life of the child is certainly lost. Relative indications shorjd therefore not exist.

The indications for therapeutic abortion may be divided into the following heads:
(1) P; i t li o 1 0 g i c conditions directly due to the pregnancy.

(2) Maternal diseases aggravated by preg- nancy.

(3) Extreme contractions of the birth canal.

(1) Of the pathologic conditions that are directly caused by the occurrence of gestation and lead to dangerous complications, we have:

A. Incarceration of the pregnant uterus that cannot be relieved except by emptying the uterus. Incarceration is most often due to retroflexion or retroversion of the gravid uterus. By means of the knee-chest posture, or by introducing into the vagina a colpeurynter filled with, oue or two pouuds of mercury (Fig. 27), the uterus can usually be brought forward. Bimanual elevation under narcosis will sometimes be necessary. Finally, Wertheim and others have felt justified in a few cases in doing a laparotomy to break up the dense adhesions that bound down the uterus. Where these measures fail or a hiparotomy is objected to, the induction of an abortion will prove necessary. And here it should be added that such an abortion is at times most difficult to produce owing to the unusually high position of the cervix. Olshausen was compelled in one such case to resort to a hysterectomy to save the patient's life.

B. Acute hydramnios may at times give rise to such marked distention of the uterus and abdomen as to endanger the patient's life. Beside the severe pain we may have cardiac insufficiency (cyanosis, dyspnoea). Here the interruption of pregnancy is absolutely necessary, as the condition grows progressively worse, and the chance of obtaining a living child is practicall nil. The slowly forming hj dramnios of the later months of pregnancy gives rise to no such symptoms and requires no such treatment.

C. Hyperemesis is one of the most frequent and important indications for tlier-apeutic abortions. Thanks to the work of Whit-ridge Williams and others, we are learning to distinguish between several forms of liyperemesis, depending on their cause. Roughly, we can speak of a non-toxic and a toxic form. The non-toxic form may be due to malpositions, to hysteria, etc. In such cases we are practically never justified in inducing an abortion. In the toxic form, which can be recognized by certain urine changes and the other general symptoms of a toxemia, we must use the various methods of elimination. But if our patient for several weeks gets progressively worse, or if she is already in a greatly debilitated condition at the first consultation, an abortion must be done at once.

Vomiting is at times brought on by the patient so as to influence the physician to hasten the emptying of the uterus. If this is suspected, the patient must be removed to a hospital and kept under constant watch. Fritsch mentions a patient who by persistent vomiting and by abstaining fi-om food lost thirty-seven pounds in four weeks. After the doctor had finally felt compelled to do an abortion, she laughingly remarked to him that she could have refrained from vomiting if she had cared to.

Wliile one has to be ou guard against such malingerers, the rule holds good that if there is a pex'sistent loss of weight for four or live weeks, together with increased rjipidity of the pulse (110-120), some fever (100-101), and diminution in the total (piantity of urine, a therapeutic abortion is positively indicated. In i)rac-tically all cases where the intervention is not made too hi to, the result of ending the gestation is an almost immediate cessation of vomiting. Where the jjhysician waits until the patient is exhausted, termiuatiou of the pregnane " accomiilishes no good. If the case is clearly of the toxic sort, with persistent loss in weight, we slionld not wjiil too long, but empty tlic uterus at once.

(1) i'he maternal diseases aggravated by pregnancy are primarily heart and kidney lesions and tuberculosis of the respiratory tract. It isn't however, the disease itself which is of importance, so much as the special exacerbations or complications tluit occur in its course, and it is these that set the indication for therapeutic abortion. It is difficult to select the opportune time for interfering with gestation. Take, for instance, tuberculosis. Certain forms, such as laryngeal tuberculosis, demand immediate interruption of pregnancy. On the other hand, we may have a process in tlic lungs that has not advanced very far and yet has been to some extent aggravated by the ir(gnancy. The weight of the patient, together with the general well-being, and the physical signs on examining the chest, must guide the physician in setting his indications. No such case dare be decided at once, unless the danger to the mother is imminent. From three to four weeks should be consumed, as a rule, in the study of the case. A vigorous attempt must always be made to alleviate the pulmonary condition by suitable hygiene and therapeusis before resorting to such extremes as the inchu-tion of abortion.

In diseases of the heart, the question is primarily one of compensation. Where cyanosis, dyspnoea, or oedema, are present, the life of the patient is certainly endangered, and, if medicines do not give prompt relief, tlie uterus must be emptied. In kidney affections it will likewise be comparatively easy to select the right moment for interference. Should there be a largepercentageof albumen, oedema, or retinitis, it would be folly to delay action.

Certain nervous and psychic diseases at times necessitate the induction of abortion. Not, however, the neurasthenias or even the cases of so-called uervous prostration. Chorea of pregnancy is a well-marked condition, apparently toxic in origin, that, unless quickly relieved, demands the interruption of pregnancy. Certain psychoses, usually in the form of melancholia or delusional insanity, may require an ending of the gestation for the relief of the mental condition.

(3) Marked Narrowing of the Birth Canal. Only when the true conjugate is less than 6 cms. does indiiction of abortion come up for consideration: In other words, onlj the cases where Cnssarian section is absolutely necessary for the deliveiy of a living child. Here the mother is entitled to decide whether or not she will submit to the performance of such an operation. As a rule, if she is in fair general condition she should be persuaded to await the end of pregnancy and have a Caesarian section performed, since statistics show that where the operative indications have been set some time ahead, this operation is attended with a very small mortality.

TVhere a fibroid or ovarian cyst, associated with ireguancy, is incarcerated in the pelvis, theie is no reason for induction of abortion, but an indication for the operative relief of these tumors. At times the pregnancy will have to be sacrificed. Where the obstruction is an inoperable cancer of the cervix there is also no justification for interference, since here the mother's life is lost anyway and every effort must be made to get a living child by Csesarian section. The operable uterine carcinomata must all be treated by immediate total hysterectomy, independent of the duration of the pregnancy.

Technique. Consultation with another physician must legally and ethically precede any induction of abortion. If the disease threatening the mother is of the sort demanding the opinion of a specialist, as, say, in psychoses or tuberculosis, such a specialist should be called in to give his diagnosis and prognosis.

Naturally the accoucheur will not resort to any of the many uncertain medicinal means for bringing on an abortion, but will use only the less dangerous and more certain mechanical means at his disposal.

Three methods deserve special mention under this head: (1) Gradual dilatation of the cervical canal with tents, bags or instruments.

(2) Tanipoiiiulc nf the cervical canal and vaiiina witli iodo- form gauze.

(3) Puncture ol tlio inoiiil)ranes, allowing the amniotic fluid to escape.

W liicli (if these methods to employ will depend largely uixm the duration of the pregnancy and the dilatability of the cervical canal. The question of whether or not there is need of urgent haste in emptying the uterus will also have to be considered. In the first tliree months, when the ovum is usually expelled as a whole, and the amniotic cavity is proportionately small, it is best to leave the membranes unruptured, and to resort to dilatation, preferably with gauze. In some instances this will have to be preceded by dilatation with Hegar's or Goodell's dilators, so as to permit the gauze to be introduced readily. From the fourth to the sixth month, on the other hand, rupture of the membranes gives quicker results. Here the sudden difference in the size of the uterine cavity through the evacuation of the amniotic fluid stimulates the uterus to contractions that eventually expel the fetus and placenta. The use of the inelastic bag to dilate the cervix and stimulate contractions lias been highly recommended (see Fig. 41).

Wlierever possible, the uterus should not be emptied at one sitting, for this is always attended with danger of hemorihage and perforation. Occasionally, however, where spontaneous expulsion is delayed over twenty-four to forty-eight hours, and the condition of the patient demands instant relief, it is best to resort to manual or instrumental aid in emptying the uterus. Usually, the former will be found to be the safer and better method, particularly where an anesthetic is tolerated.

In the after care of these cases the same precautions must be observed as after spontaneous abortion. The patient should remain in bed from ten days to two weeks to give full opportunity for the uterus to return to its normal condition.

Prevention of Conception. Since certain conditions rare, to be sure, but none the less present justify the induction of abortion, it must of necessity be our aim in such cases to prevent a repetition of the endangering pregnancy. The simplest and most certain means of preventing such a repetition of pregnancy is the resection of the Fallopian tubes; but only in certain instances is the obstetrician justified in performing this operation. This subject was the occasion of a very earnest discussion at the meeting of the American Gynecological Society held in 1909 at New York. Green and others maintained that such an operation was never justified. The majority, howevei, seemed to feel that it was that the woman's life should not be again imperiled by Caesarian section if she desired to be relieved of this danger. Resection of the tubes is employed as a routine prophylactic measure in operations for total prolapse, where the uterus is sutured into the vesicovaginal septum in women still within the child-bearing period.

Hyperemesis, chorea, acute hydramnios, incarcerated uterus, would not justify such sterilizing measures, as they are not likely to be repeated in subsequent pregnancies. On the other hand, certain selected cases of tuberculosis, heart disease, and particularly psychoses, may justify resection of the tubes as a preventive measure.

Obliteration of the uterine cavity, termed "uterine castration," has l)een recommended for these cases by Pincus. This obliteration is accomplished by means of the injection of superheated steam. There are, however, other means of preventing conception beside the sterilizing oijeratious. These measures are none of them certain except total sexual abstinence, which is rarely practicable. That a life of continued celibacy is not harmful to any human being has been amply proven. Among persons who are somewhat older and i os-sessed of sufficient self-control, celibacy is of course the best means of preventing conception.

AVitli the vast majority of persons, however, this is impossible, and here we must resort to other measures. There is a natural reluctance on the part of physicians and text-books to discuss this subject, since it is apt to lead to abuses in one way or another. And yet, this very refusal on the part of the profession to speak of these subjects has led to the most serious mistakes and injurious practices on the part of their patients. The gratification of the sexual impulse is not a crime, and the mere fact that an effort is made to prevent the coitus from resulting in a pregnancy that may endanger the mother's life does not constitute an immoral act. There has been much prudery and prejudice in the views of Americans on this subject. Leaving aside for the present any consideration of the eases where, for social reasons, such as poverty, drunkenness ou the part of tlie husband, etc., a iurther pregnancy is undesirable, there is a whole series of cases, as already mentioned, where tlie mother's life would be directly endangered. Here we not only have the right, but it seems to me it is our duty to tell the married couple what precautious can be used to prevent conception. This is doubly necessary, inasmuch as these persons, if left to themselves, would resort to more dangerous and less certain measures.

Of these dangerous measures coitus iuterruptus is the one most fiequently practiced. The withdrawal of the organ at the moment of ejaculation leads in time to chronic congestion of the oigans of reproduction and to certain nervous disturbances, often of a serious character. The stem pessary as a means of preventing conception is so liable to load to infection of the uterine cavity that it ought never be used. Moreover, it is, in fact, rather an abortifacient than a means of avoiding conception. There are a number of other measures that are not usually harmful and in the vast majority of cases will result in facultative sterility. Intermenstrual intercourse will certainly limit the chances of the occurrence of a pregnancy considerably. From the tenth day after the cessation of menstruation to five days before the onset of the next period is the time when fecundation is least likely to occur. The taking of douches immediately post coitum with an astringent solution such as dilute acetic acid or aluminum acetate (1 drachm to 2 quarts of water) or liquor alumini acetatis (VL ounce to 1 quart) will greatly decrease the chances of conception. Such douching must, however, be restricted, for, if done at frequent intervals, it may lead to circulatory disturbances of the uterus. A means for injecting the antiseptic astringent solution duiing the time of ejaculation, called Venus-douche, has been devised in Germany and would seem to be rather effective. The effect of such an astringent on spermatozoa is immediate. All movements cease at once and disintegration takes place rapidly.

The use of vaginal suppositories or sponges has been recommended. Antiseptic astringent substances are used as ingredients for them in order to obtain the desired effect. Corrosive sublimate has been extensively employed, but is no more effective than less poisonous substances. I have seen several severe burns and salivation produced by the insertion of a bichloride tablet in the vagina for the purpose of preventing conception.

Soft-rubber appliances to prevent the entrance of the spermatic fluid into the uterine cavity have the disadvantage that they are liable to tear, but otherwise are largely employed to prevent conception. The condom, so commonly employed by men, must be made of a good quality of rubber. The soft rubber shield fastened to a pessary which is used abroad by women to cover the entrance of the uterus, and is known as the Mensinga pessary, is less secure than the condom and necessitates frequent removal and replacement by a physician. Hence, it is not to be recommended.

In general, therefore, we may advise in these rare cases of organic disease of the woman, that if intercourse cannot be absolutely prohibited, it should be restricted to a minimiim; it should be observed in the intermenstrual period, with a rubber protective to the male organ and an astringent douche afterwards on the part of the wife.

Ergot and Its Preparations

Of all the medicines employed in tlie treatiiieut of ubortions, ergot is uuquestiouably the most important. During the past fifteen years pharmacologists have done much to make its administration safer and more efficient. It has, therefore, seemed advisable to me to add a short chapter reviewing tlie principal preparations that have been put upon the market, particularly because obstetrical writers have not heretofore given the subject due consideration.

Ergot or secale coriiutum is the compact mycelium of the fungus Claviceps i urpurea, growing upon rye. It is chiefly exported from Kussia, Austria, German and Spain. In the middle ages, when the presence of ergot upon the grain was not understood, bread or other food stuffs made from such grain gave rise to the most serious poisoning. The disease known as St. Anthony's fire, very common in those days, and often resulting in death, was unquestionably due to the ingestion of large quantities of ergot of rye.

Many of these toxic symptoms were, however, due to associated substances, and not to the essential alkaloid, ergotiu. The earliest known allusion to the action of ergot upon the uterus was made by Lonicer in 1582. It was not until the eighteenth century that it was more extensively used in obstetrical cases. Ilosack was the first American to recommend its use, early in the nineteenth century.

Special importance attends the efforts to purify the preparations of ergot. The necessity for such efforts were: (1) The absence of standard preparations of constant strength.

(2) The frequency of abscess formation and severe local irritation when the drug was used hypodermically.

In 1894 Kobert was able to isolate three substance out of ergot: ergotinic acid, sphacelinic acid and an alkaloid which he called cor-nutin. The essential therapeutic action, according to his tests, lay in the sphacelinic acid. Jacoby, in 1897, was able to isolate a sub- stance similar in properties to spbaeeliuic acid, only more powerful, whicli he termed s p li a c e l o t o x i u. Unfortunately, however, this product was found to be very unstable and hence was not practical for general use. The work of Keller supported in general the conclusions of Robert. Tlie pure crystalline alkaloid apparently had no therapeutic value. In 1902 Palm published his extensive investigations. They showed that many of the preparations at that time upon the market were not essentially different, since they depended for their effect upon the presence of sphacelotoxin. The substances tested included Cornutin Robert, Ergotin Tanred, Cornutin Erg. Bombelon, Ergotin Denzel, Ergot Aseptic Parke, Davis Co.

Additional refinements in the manufacture of these prodiicts have since been made, aud the following preparations can be recommended as reliable and safe for hypodermic use.

Ergone (Parke, Davis Co.), a brownish liquid which in contradistinction to Ergot Aseptic is half as concentrated, and is not put up in separate glass globules for hypodermic use, but can nevertheless be thus used, since it contains a sufficient quantity of an antiseptic, chloretone, to keep it free of bacterial decomposition. Several samjiles of ergone exposed in open and closed bottles were examined and found to have remained entirely sterile. Ergone is free from ergotinic acid. Its relationship to sphacelotoxin is not explained. Dosage, fifteen to thirty drops hypodermically.

Ernutin (Burroughs, Wellcome Co., England) is the hydrate of the crystalline alkaloid, ergotinine. This product is chemically termed ergotoxine. According to Barger and Carr, who have done the experimental work for this company, ergotoxine is readily standardized and sterile. They claim it is an even purer preparation than sphacelotoxin. Dosage of Ernutin, as it is commercially termed, is five to ten drops, contained in hermetically sealed glass phials for hypodermic use.

Secacornin (F. Hoffmann-Laeoche Co., Basel), does not contain eri; otinic acid or sphacelinic acid, but contains the alkaloid, cornutin, loosely associated with substances related to sphacelotoxin. It is based upon Ergotin Keller. Keller turned over the manufacture of this preparation to the Basel firm and permitted the change of name to Secacornin. Its therape itic efficiency has been amply tested in the clinics abroad. It comes in sterile her- metically sealed phials for hypodermic use, each phial containing fifteen drops, equivalent to four grams of Secale cornutum. The dose is seven to fifteen drops hypodermically.

For internal administration, ergotol, ergone and the U. S. P. fluid extract will be found reliable and non-irritatinff.

Abortion, causes, 26 diagnosis, 48 cervical, 36, 37 complete, definition, 42 diagnosis, 47 treatment, 83 complicated, 3 criminal, diagnosis, 48 frequency, 78 prevention, 78 death from, 3 definition, 2 diagnosis, 38, 39 differential diagnosis, 51 disease due to mismanaged, 1 etiology, 2G frequency, 3 habitual, 5 increase in number, 3 incomplete, definition, 42 diagnosis, 43 inevitable, diagnosis, 41, 42, 43 symptoms, 34

Tarnier's sign, 43 infected, 3 missed, 152 necessity for registration, 81 odium attached to name, 2 operative indications, 88 prevention, 61 prognosis, 58 public record of all, 81 recent, definition, 42 diagnosis, 47 registration of, to diminish instrumental interference, 80 spontaneous, 3 syphilis as a cause, 5 therapeutic, 1G2 threatened, diagnosis, 41, 42 prevention, 75 symptoms, 34 uncomplicated, treatment, 82 Active treatment of abortions, 88 Acute yellow atrophy, causing abortion, 30 Adherence of ovum to uterus, cause, 19 Adherent placenta, cause, 18 Adhesions, breaking, during pregnancy, 69 stretching of, in pregnancy, 63 uterine, causing abortion, 28 Admission of evidence, criminal abortion, 80 After-treatment of abortions, 85 Albuminuria, following placental infarct, 23 Alcohol in sepsis, 141

Alcoholism, producing congenital inanition of fetus, 31
Amenorrhoea, diagnostic value, in pregnancy, 38
Amnion, covering fetus in abortions, 17 cysts, 24 intact, 19
Amniotic adhesions, causing fetal death, 31
Amniotic cavity, formation during first month, 10
Anatomy of early pregnancy, 7
Anemia, after hemorrhage, treatment, 126 of mother, producing fetal death, 31
Anesthetic in intrauterine examination, 46
Angioma of placenta, 24
Antigen, 66
Antisepsis, influence on frequency criminal abortion, 78. 79
Anti-toxin, streptococcus, in sepsis, 140
Anthrax, fetal, causing death, 32
Apoplexy, placental, 22
Asafoetida, prophylactic against abortion, 73
Asepsis, influence on frequency criminal abortion, 78 79
Aseptic precautions, for intra-uterine examination, 46
Bacteriolysin. 65
Bag dilator, inelastic, manner of Introduction. 108 Bed. rest in, after abortion, 86 Bicornuate pregnant uterus, diff. diagn.

from perforation, 147 Bimanual examination in tubal abortion, 57 Bleeding, see Hemorrhage in abortion, 34 in digital removal of placenta, 115 in tubal abortion, 54 Blood, injections into, in sepsis, 140 Blood-clot, differentiation from chorionic villus, 45 in uterus, differentiation from ovum, 46 Blood-poisoning, education as to danger, in criminal abortion, 79 Blood-spaces, connection of ovum with, of the mother, 17 Blow, causing abortion, 28 Brush, description of, used in ecouvillon- nage, 121 Brushing out the uterus, 121

Cancer of uterus, differentiation from abortion,
Capillaries, maternal, atlarkeil by tiopho- blast. 9 Cases, seletted, 2
Castration, uterine, to prevent conception, 167 Causes ot abortion, 2G diagnosis, 48 Causes of frequency of abortion in spconl and third month. 5 Cervical abortion. Sti, 37 Cervical dilatation to induce abortion, 1G5 Cervical tears, cayising abortion, 2(i. 123 in digital removal of placenta, 117 I)rognosis after, (0 repair of, ()2 Cervix, amputation of, causing abortion. 26 dilatation, in abortion, 35. technique. 105 with gauze. 106 with metal dilator, 106 with inelastic bag, 107 retraction of. due to ergot.

83 Change in nutrition of fetus causing abortion, 5 Cholera, fetal, producing death, 32 Chorea gravidarum, producing abortion. 30 indicating therapeutic abortion, 165 Chorio-epithelioma. 24, 53 following hydatid mole, 160 Chorioma, 160 Chorion, anatomy of. 9 cysts of, 24 frondosum, 12 formation of, 9 laeve. 12 Chorionic villi, diagnosis of, 45 diagnostic value of. in abortion, 41 diagnostic value in criminal abortion.

49 growth into maternal veins, 12 Chorionitis. suppurative, 23 Circulatory changes, periods of. 7 Classification of causes of abortion, objections to. 26, 27 Clotting of blood, diagnostic value, 34 Cold, applications of. in threatened abortion. 76 Collargolum, injection of. in sepsis, 141 Complement. 65

Completed abortion, diagnosis, 47 Complications of abortions, frequency of, 3 prognosis. 59 prophylaxis of, 88 Conception, prevention of, 166 in anemia of parents. 64 by pelvic inflammation, 6 prophylaxis before, 61 Confessed criminal abortion. 5 Confinements, ratio of abortions to. 4 Congenital inanition, resulting in fetal death. 31 Connection of ovum to mother in first six weeks, 17 during second six weeks. 17

Conservative treatment of abortions, 88 Consistency of aborting uterus, 46 Constipation, causing abortion, 26, 28, 73 prevention of, 68 Contraction-ring of uterus, in retaineij placenta. 113, 114 Coitus, causing abortion, 26 during pregnancy. 68 frequent, causing congenital inanition. 31 iuterruptus, 168 Counter-pressure, abdominal, to prevent perforation, 149 Course of abortion, in variation with stage of pregnancy, 36 Criminal abortion, admission of evidence. 80 confession of, 5 diagnosis, 48 education, 79 frequency of, 3, 5, 78 importance ot increase, 79 in married and unmarried, 5 instruments used in, 78 legislation. 80 microscopic examination of uterus in, 48 mortality after. 58, 59 pievention, 78 by registration of all abortions, 80 rarity of convictions, 80 rarity of prosecutions, 80 registration of midwives, 80 sepsis after, frequency of, 58 Crackling, diagnostic value in incomplete abortion. 46 Curage. technique of. 109-117 Curettage, instruments for, 120 in hydatid mole. 161 in missed abortion, 155 in sepsis. 142 in tubal abortion. 54, 55 necessity of. after abortion, 25 technique of, 120 Curette, as cause of perforation, 145, 14(blunt, in sepsis, 136 objection to. in sepsis, 135

Orthmann. 136.

spoon. Martin's. 94 use of, in abortions. 121

Dancing, causing abortion, 28

Deaths from abortion. 3

Death of fetus, causing abortion, 31, 43 diagnosis of, 43 manner of causing abortion, 27 Decidua. agglutination of, 15 basilaris. 10 capsularis. 10 compacta. 10 diagnostic value in pregnancy. 40 differential diagnosis. 40 expulsion of. during first six weeks; pregnancy. 16 formation, 9 liquefaction of, 24 nuclei of,

Decidua, ovum extruded from, 16 persistence of, 25 proliferation, 10 reflexa, 10, 15 growth of, 12 removed digitally, 17 retained, outline of treatment, 131 serotina, 10 shreddy discharge of, 18 spongiosa, 10 vera, 10 Decidual cast of uterine cavity, 16 Deciduitis, chronic hyperplastic, 24 polyposa, 24 suppurative, 24 Decomposition producing fever, 35 Definition of abortion, 2 Degeneration, calcareous, of placenta, 23 Development in pregnancy, stages of, 7 Development of embryo, 13 Diabetes, cause of abortion, 29 Diagnosis of abortion, 38, 39 of pregnancy. 38 Differential diagnosis of abortion and cancer uterus, 52 and fibroid tumor of uterus, 51 and hemorrhagic endometritis, 50 and irregular menses. 50 and tubal pregnancy, 53 of blood-clot and ovum in utero. 46 and villus, 45 of chorio-epithelioma and cancer, 53 of threatened and inevitable abortion, 42 Difliculty in diagnosis abortion, 38 Digital removal, difliculty of, 114 technique. 109-117 with two fingers, 132 Dilatation, cervical, for intra-uterine examination, 46 technique, 105 with inelastic bag, 107 Dilator, Hegar's metal, 100 cause of uterine perforation. 144 proper use of. 150 uterine, Goodell's, 93 Discharge in abortion. 35 Douche, astringent, to prevent conception, 168 intra-uterine, in curettement, 121 in sepsis, 138 technique, 122 vaginal, after abortions. 86 cause of abortion. 29 in uncomplicated abortion. 82. 84 in hemorrhage. 123 in sepsis, 135. 137, 138 Douche-can, for instrument case, 93 Douche-nozzle, description of intrauterine, 122 Duration of bleeding in inevitable abortion. 43 Duration of pregnancy, diagnosis, 47 Dysmenorrhoea membranacea, 50

Eclampsia, cause of abortion, 30 Ecouvillonnage, technique. 121 in sepsis, 136

Ectopic pregnancy (see tubal abortion), 53 Education on beginning of life in utero, 79 danger of blood poisoning in criminal abortion, 79 Ejaculation of spermatozoa into vagina. 7 Embryo, bending of, 13 cylindrical, 21 development of, 10 Emmenagogues, causing abortion, 29 Endometritis, following abortion. 25 hemorrhagic, differentiation from abortion. 50. 51 post-abortum. 25. 44 preventing conception, 6 treatment of. preventing abortion, fii Ergone. 86, 125, 171 Ergot. 170 after abortion. S6 causing abortion, 29 hypodermic use of, 86 in threatened abortion. 77 in uncomplicated abortion, 83 Ergotin, 170. 171 Ergotol. 86 Ergotoxine. 171 Ernutin. 86. 125. 171 Erysipelas, fetal, causing death, 32 Evidence, admission of, in criminal abortion. 80 Exciting causes of abortion, 26 Exo-coelom cavity. 10 Expectant treatment of abortions, 89 Exploration, digital, of uterus. 113 Expression of ovum. Budin, 99. Ill Hoening, 100 with uterus anteverted, 100 with uterus retroverted, 99 Expulsion of ovum, complete, cause of, 17 from seventh to twelfth week, 17 manner of. 18 pre-viable. 2 Expulsion of placenta, interval before, in early pregnancy, 130 External genitals, applications to, resulting in abortion. 30

Failure to prevent abortion, proportion of, 75 Fall, causing abortion, 28 Fetal death, diagnosis of. 43 due to decidual hyperplasia, 25 due to syphilis. 5 Fetus, change in nutrition of. causing abortion, 5 covered by amnion, expulsion of, 17 death of. causing abortion,27 decomposed by bacteria, 21 development of, 15 macerated. 21 microscopic examination to determines presence of. 41 pathology of, 21 sanguinolentus, 21 softening of, 21 Fever, after c irettage of abortion. 35 in inevitable abortion,

Fever, in sapremia, 133 in tubal abprtion, 55 Fibrinous areas in placenta, 14 Fibroid uterus, differentiation from abortion, 51 differentiation from missed abortion, 154 Finger, introduction of, in digital removal, 109111 perforation of uterus by. 14G Fixation of ovum to uterus, 11 Fofceps, ovum, description, 94 placental, technique of removal with, 117 Formaldehjde injections in blood in sepsis, 140 Fowler position, 142 France, decrease in population of, 3 Frequency of abortion, to duration of pregnancy, 4 in second and third month, cause of, 5 statistics, 4 in third month, due to syphilis, 5 causes of. 5 due to criminal attempts, 5 Frequency of criminal abortions, 5 Fright, cause of abortion. 30

Gauze tamponade in sepsis, 139 Germany, increase in population of, 3 Gestation, see Pregnancy, 17 Glands, hyperplasia of, in pregnancy, 25

Habitual abortions. 5 prevention of. 73 prognosis, 60 Heart disease, indication for therapeutic abortion. 164 treatment preventing abortion, 69 Heat, application of, in threatened abortion. 76 dry. in sepsis. 139 Heavy lifting, causing abortion, 28 Hematoma-mole, formation of, 157 prognosis and treatment, 159 Hemolysin, 65 Hemolysis, technique of. 66 Hemorrhage, see Bleeding cause of. 123 immediate treatment of. 123, 124 in inevitable abortion, 34 in perforation, treatment. 150 prognosis after. 59 symptoms of, in abortion, 123 Hospital, advantages, for obstetrical operations. 99 necessity for, in tubal abortion, 55 records of frequency of abortions, 4 Hour glass contraction of uterus. 113. 114 Hydatid mole. 159 cause fetal death, 32 symptoms. 159 treatment, 101 Hydramnios, acute, causing abortion. 28 indication for therapeutic abortion, 163 Hydramnios-ovum. 153

Hydrastis, 87

Hyperemesis, cause of abortion, 30 indication for therapeutic abortion, 163 Hyperemia, passive, in sepsis, 139 Hyperplasia, glandular, in abortion, 25 Hyperpyrexia, cause of abortion, 30, 31, 32 Hysterectomy for ijerforation of uterus, 151 in sepsis, 143 Impregnation, occurrence of, 7 Implantation of ovum in uterus. 7 Incarceration of pregnant uterus, 70, 162 Incomplete abortion, diagnosis, 43 digital examination, 45 Induction of abortion, methods of, 166 Inelastic bag. use of. 108 Inevitable abortion, diagnosis, 41. 42, 43

Tarnier's sign, 43 Infarct, anemic, 22 cause of. 22. 23 causing albuminuria. 23 placental, 22 Infected abortions, 3 Infectious diseases of mother causing abortion, 30 Inflammation of chorion, 23 Injections into blood, in sepsis, 140 Instrument case, 91 Instrumental abortion, more frequent at second and third month, 5 mortality after. 58, 59 Instrumentarium. 91 Instruments, dangerous, use of, causing perforation, 149 Intervillous spaces, decreased size In syphilis, 24 primary, 9 secondary, 11 Intestines, injury to, in perforation, 145 resection of, in perforation, 151 Intra-uterine douche, technique, 122 Intra-uterine digital exploration, 46 Iodoform gauze, dangers of. in tamponade, 100 Iron tonics, in anemia. 64 Irrigator, uterine. Bozeman. 93 Irrigation, continuous uterine, in sepsis. 138 dangers of, in perforation. 151 Irritation, mechanical, causing abortion, 28 nerve, cause of abortion. 30 thermic, causing abortion. 29 toxic, causing abortion, 29

Kidney disease, indication for therapeutic abortion, 164 treatment, preventing abortion. 69 Kitchen table, arrangement for operations. 98 disadvantages in operative work, 98 Knee-chest position, 70, 72

Laminaria tent, 106

Langhans cells, disappearance of. 14

Lanugo, time of formation of.

Laparotomy, causing aboition, 28 for perforation, 151 Lead poisoning, cause of abortion, 29 Local applications in sepsis, 138

Maceration, degrees of, 21 production of, in fetus, 21 Malaria, producing abortion, 32 Malthusian theory, frequency of abortion in relation to, 3 Massage of uterus in hemorrhage, 124 Material expelled, examination for presence of fetus. 4-i microscopic examination, 40 Measles, cause of abortion, 32 Membranes, circulatory disturbances in, 22 degenerations of, 22 intact during abortion, 18 pathology of. 22 rupture of, causing retained placenta, 18 in uncomplicated abortion, 82 to induce abortion, 166 Menstrual period, precautions during, to prevent abortion, 68 predisposition to abortion at. 26 Menstruation, delayed, differentiation of abortion from, 6 irregular, differentiation from abortion. 50 Mercury, administration of, to prevent abortion, 65 Mercury pressure treatment in retro-verted gravid uterus, 71, 163 Microscopic diagnosis of pregnancy, 40 Microscopic examination, in recent abortion. 47 in tubal abortion, 56 Midwives, registration of, to decrease abortions. 80 Miscarriage, definition of. 2 Misplacements, uterine, causing abortion.

28 Missed abortion, 152 calcareous degeneration in, 23 causes of, 153 clinical course, 153 pathology of, 152 treatment. 154 Mole, blood, 156 Breus. 157 carneous, 156 fleshy, 150 hematoma. 157 hydatid. 24. 159 causing fetal death, 32 Mole pregnancy. 6. 150 calcareous degeneration in, 23 Monstrosities, fetal, producing death, 31 Month of pregnancy, frequency of abortion to, 4 Morbidity after abortions, 58, 59 Mortality after abortions, 58 Mother, physical condition of, causing fetal death, 31

Narcosis for digital removal. 109 Narrow pelvis, indication for therapeutic abortion, 165 Nasal applications, causing abortion. 30 National danger of increased frequency of abortion, 3 Nervous diseases indicating therapeutic abortion, 164 Nucleus of decidua-cell, 9 Nursing, causing uterine contractions, 30 Nutrition of fetus, at third month, causing abortion, 5 interference with, causing death, 31

Obstetrics, inefficiency of textbooks on, 1 Omentum, prolapse of, in perforation, 145 Operations during pregnancy, 09, 70 for septic abortions. 141 general preparations for, in abortion cases, 97 Operative measures, frequency of, 1 Opiates, use of, in threatened abortion, 76 Opinions of other obstetricians. 1 Outline of treatment in abortion. 131 Ovarian tumor, causing abortion, 28 Ovisac retained, outline of treatment. 131 Ovum, connection with maternal tissues, 17, 19 differentiation from bloodclot in iiter-us, 46 expelled intact, 16 expression of, Budin, 99 Hoening, 100 extruded from decidua, 16 imbedding of, 7 manner of expulsion of, 18 palpation of. in abortion, 39 retained, outline of treatment, 131 Ovum forceps, see Placental forceps causing perforation, 145, 146, 149 description. 94 different kinds of. 149 technique to prevent perforation. 150

Packer, gauze, use in uterine tamponade. 102 uterine, for abortions, 93 Pain, causing abortion, 30 cessation of. diagnostic value, 35 character of, in abortion. 35 in abortion. 34 in tubal abortion, 54 relief of. in sepsis, 137 Paris, frequency of abortions in, 3 Pathology of abortion, 16 Pathology of fetus, memljranes and decidua, 21 Pelvic abscess. 142 Pelvic exudates, treatment bv drv heat, 139 Pelvic inflammation preventing conception, 6 Percentage of abortions in second and third month. 5 Perforation, danger of, in retained abortion, 60 diagnosis of, 146 differential diagnosis,

Perforation, (iiffcrcniiatioii from souiul-ing Fallopian tulios. 14S frequpn-. v of. 144 in criminal abortion, SO manner of, 144 symptoms of, 140 treatment of, 150 uterine, causes of, 148 Periods of circulatory changes, 7 Pessary, intra-uterine, 5, 168 introduction of, 63, 64 Mensinga, 169 pressure necrosis after. 72 in retroverted gravid uterus, 72 time of removal, in pregnancy, 72 Physiological classification of causes of abortion, 28 Placenta, cause of delayed expulsion, IS circulatory changes causing abortion.

5 digital removal, technique, 109-117 dimensions of, 14 fibrinous areas in, 14 growth of, during third to fifth month, 14 infarct of, 22 loosened pieces, removal of, 117 loosening of, with forceps, 119 polyp of, 25 relation to uterine cavity of, 14 retained, causes, 127 syphilis of, 23 syphilitic, size of, 24 tumors of, 24, when it is right to call it retained, 130 Placental apoplexy, 22 Placental forceps, see Ovum forceps precautions necessary, 117-120 technique of removal by, 117 Placental thrombosis, causing abortion, 2fi Plague, fetal, causing death, 32 Pneumonia, fetal, producing death. 32 Polyclinic records of frequency of abortions, 4 Polyp, placental. 25 Population, relative decrease in France over Germany, 3 Potassium iodide, prophylactic against abortion, 65, 73 Practitioner, operative indications for, 90 Predisposing causes of abortion, 26 Pregnancy, anatomy of first half of, 7 diagnosis of, 3S duration, diagnosis, 47 prophylaxis of abortion during, 67 ratio of abortion to, 3 Pressure due to retroversion causing abortion, 5 Pressure necrosis after use of pessary, 72 Pressure weight treatment in retroverted gravid uterus. 71 Prevention of abortion, 61 Pre-viable expulsion of ovum, 2 Prognosis of abortion, 58 Prolapse of omentum through perforation opening, 145 Il-olouged rest in threatened abortion. 76 Prophylaxis before conception, 61 Psychic nerve irritation, 30 Pulse in tubal abortion, 55 Pus-tubes after abortion, 142

Railroad journey, causing abortion, 28 Reaction, Wassermann, technique of, 65 Recent abortion, diagnosis, 47 microscopic examination in, 47 Reflex nerve irritation cause of abortion.

30 Relaxation of uterine muscle, diff. diagn.

from perforation, 147 Removal of placenta, digital, technique.

109-117 Resection of tiibes to prevent conception 167 Rest in bed. after aliortions, 85 preventing abortion, 68. 76 Rest, mental, in threatened abortion. 77 Retained ovum, outline of treatment. 131 Retained placenta, 17 cause, 127 decomposition. 127 definition, 130 diagnosis, 43 due to ergot, 84 due to rupture of ovisac, 18 expectative treatment, 83 frequency, 127 microscopic changes in, 127 outline of treatment. 131 pathology of. 127, 128 prognosis after, 59 Retroversion of uterus, causing abortion at third month, 5 correction during pregnancy, 70 incarcerated, 162 spontaneous correction in pregnancy, 62, 63 Retinal pigment, diagnostic value of, 41 Retraction, of cervix, due to ergot, 83 Riding, causing abortion, 28 Rubber gloves, use in abortions, 97

Sapremia, 133 symptoms of, 133 treatment of, 133 Scarlet fever, fetal, causing death, 32 Sea-baths, producing abortion, 29 Seca-cornin, 86, 171 Sepsis. 133 fever in severe, 136 frequency, criminal abortion, 80 . general measures in treatment. 136 local measures in. 137 objections to sharp curette, 135 operative treatment. 141 physical examination, 134 prognosis after, 59 reasons for frequency, 133 severe form. 136 treatment by ecouvillonage. 121 treatment of mild cases, 134 use of curette, 134, 135 use of ovum forceps.

Septic venous thrombosis, operation for, 143 Sewing machine, worli, cause of abortion, 68 Silver in colloid solution, injections of, 141 Sitz-bath, producing abortion,

29 Smallpox, cause of abortion. 30 fetal, producing death. 32 prevention, during pregnancy, 69 Sounding Fallopian tubes, diff. diagn.
from perforation, 148 Speculum, in position, 96 operating, self-retaining, 95 vaginal. Graves, 95 Spermatozoa, ejaculation of. into vagina, 7 Sphacelotoxin, 171 Spirochaeta pallida, 23, 65 Spontaneous abortions, prognosis, 58 Stage of abortion, diagnosis of. 41 Stages of development in i)regnancy, 7 Stage of pregnancv, ratio of abortions to.
4 Staining of decidua cells, 9 Statistics on frequency of abortion, 3, 4 Steam, superheated, in uterus, 139 Streptococcus anti-toxin in sepsis. 140 Strumous parents, treatment, preventing abortion, 69 Stypticin. 29, 87 Styptol. S7 Sub-involution of uterus. 25 after abortion. 85 Suppurative chorlonitis, 23 Supra-renal extract in abortion, 87 Syncytium, 9 presence of, in material examined, 41 Syphilis, blood-serum diagnosis, 65 blood vessels in, 24 causing abortion in third month, 5 cause of macerated fetus, 21 diagnosis as cause of abortion, 48 fetal, causing abortion, 32 objections to theory that it causes abortion at third month, 5 of placenta, 23, 24 treatment of, before conception,-65 during pregnancy, 68 Syphilitic infarct, 23
Tamponade, cervical, to induce abortion, 166 general precautions, 100 in hemorrhage, 124 uterine, gauze packer for, 102 indications for, 101 in sepsis. 138 technique, 101, 102 vaginal, in threatened abortion, 76 in uncomplicated abortion, 82 technique, 100, 101 Temperament, as cause of abortion, 26 Temperature in uterus higher than that of mother, 32 Tenaculum forceps, see volsella, 93
Text-books on obstetrics, inefficiency of. 1 Therapeutic abortion, indications for, 162 technique, 105 Thermophore bags, in sepsis, 139 Third month, frequency of abortions in, 5 Threatened abortion, diagnosis, 41 prevention, 75 proportion of failures to prevent, 75 Thrombo-phlebitis, septic, operation for, 143 Thrombosis, of maternal or fetal vessels, 22 septic, of veins, operation for, 143 Tooth, extraction of, causing abortion, 30 Toxemia, placental, causing abortion, 30 Treatment, outline of, in abortion, 131 Trophoblast, activity of, 9 Tubal abortion, combination with intrauterine abortion, 56 differential diagnosis from intra-uter-ine abortion, 53, 54, 55, 57 examination findings in, 55 microscopic findings, 56 Tuberculosis, fetal, causing death, 32 indicating therapeutic abortion, 164 Typhoid, fetal, producing death. 32
Umbilical cord, formation of, 11 lengthening of, 12 twist, causing fetal death. 32 Unguentum, Crede. in sepsis, 141 Uterine cavity, depth of, 10 relation of ovum to, 10 Uterine glands, proliferation during pregnancy, 10 Uterine segment, formation of lower, 13 Uterine tamponade, indications for, 101 technique, 101, 102 Uterine wall, softness, predisposing to perforation, 149 Uterus, adhesions of, causing abortion, 28 circulatory changes in, causing abortion, 5 contraction-ring in retained placenta, 113, 114 incarcerated pregnant, 162 increase in size of, during pregnancy, 13, 15 physical examination of, during abortion, 36 retroversion of, correction in pregnancy, 63

Vaginal incision of pelvic abscess, 142
Vaginal tamponade, technique. 100, 101
Vaporization in sepsis, 139
Veins, maternal, dilated bv chorionic villi, 12
Viburnum as prophylactic against abortion, 73
Volsella punctures, diagnostic value in criminal abortion, 48

Volsellum, 93 use of, in digital removal. 109-111
Wassermann blood-reaction, 65
Page
Aionson 141
Augustiu 148
Barger 171
Barnes 107
Boldt 42,130
Bombelon 171
Bozeman 93
Braun 88,107
Bieus 156, 157
Bryce 45
Budin 88, 99, 111,135
Bumm 10, 13, 39, 54, 72, 143, IGO
Can- 171
Casteran 88
Champetier-de-Ribes 107, 108.150
Chazan 4,48,101
Crede 117, 141
Crossen 14, G3, 64, 70, 119,120
Doederlein.-. 88
Dohrn 88
Doleris 3, 78
Doi-sett 81
Duehrssen 88,101
Duncan 152
Eden 22
Edgar. 9, 14, 76, 77, 88, 159
Etheridge 88
Fehling 88
Fraenkel 153
Franz 5
Fritsch 163
Garrigues 88
Gellhorn 140
Glasgow 94
Goodell 93.160
Graefe 153
Graves 93,95
Green 167
Guillemeau 22
Halban 150
Hartmann 145
Hegar 39, 144, 150.166

Heineck 144, 146,151
V. Herff 138
Hirst 88
Hitschman 25
Hoening 100
HoiI 46
Hosack 170
Jacoby 170
Keller 171
Kelly 96
Keyssner 4
Kleinwaeohter 77,132
Kneise 4
Robert 170,171
Kiiestner 75
Page I. anghans 9, 14
Lomer 73
Lonicer 170
Lusk 88
Marchand 159
Marmorek 141
Martin 94
Maygrier 59
Mcgregory 88
Mensinga 169
Michailoff 4
Moebius 130
Montgomery 52
Mundfi 88
Murphy 126
Nassauer 149
Newell 88
Olshausen 163
Opitz 25
Orthmann 121, 134,149
Palm 171
Parvin 88
Pinard 9
Pincus 139,167
Playtair 88
Ploess 78
Polano 139
Pozzi 88
Reynolds 77, 88
Rimette 3. 58,127

Sanders 79
Schultze 149
Sims 86
Sittner 59,127
Smith. A. 72
Stumpf 88
Tanred 171
Tarnier 43, 88
Taylor 69
Thomas, T. G 1, 5, 29, 35, 58, 68, 88, 97
Treub 5, 58
Tussenbroek 147
Virchow 159
Voorhees 107,150
Waldeyer 11
Ward 86, 88, 89,132
Warthin 24, 25
Wassermann 65
Webster 83, 88
Werelius 146
Wertheim 52. 157,163
Williams 23. 88.163
V. Winckel 22, 23, 41, 48, 78. 88
Winter H9
Zweifel 88

PLEASE DO NOT REMOVE CARDS OR SLIPS FROM THIS POCKET
UNIVERSITY OF TORONTO LIBRARY